ROMANCING THE FUTURE

DEAREMY ♡
HERE'S TO ROMANCING
TO YOUR
FEATURE!
LOVE,
JEOUP
07/08

green press
INITIATIVE

Findhorn Press is committed to preserving ancient forests and natural resources. We elected to print this title on 30% post consumer recycled paper, processed chlorine free. As a result, for this printing, we have saved:

14 Trees (40' tall and 6-8" diameter)
5,723 Gallons of Wastewater
11 million BTU's of Total Energy
735 Pounds of Solid Waste
1,379 Pounds of Greenhouse Gases

Findhorn Press made this paper choice because our printer, Thomson-Shore, Inc., is a member of Green Press Initiative, a nonprofit program dedicated to supporting authors, publishers, and suppliers in their efforts to reduce their use of fiber obtained from endangered forests.

For more information, visit www.greenpressinitiative.org

Environmental impact estimates were made using the Environmental Defense Paper Calculator. For more information visit: www.papercalculator.org.

ROMANCING THE FUTURE

By

Judy Julin

with

Gina Mazza Hillier

FINDHORN PRESS

First published by Findhorn Press 2008
ISBN: 978-1-84409-129-4

British Library Cataloguing-in-Publication Data. A catalogue record for this book is available from the British Library.

Cover design by Damian Keenan
Layout by e-BookServices.com
Printed and bound in America

1 2 3 4 5 6 7 8 9 10 11 12 13 14 13 12 11 09 08

Published by
Findhorn Press
305A The Park,
Findhorn, Forres
Scotland IV36 3TE
Tel +44(0)1309 690582
Fax +44(0)1309 690036
eMail info@findhornpress.com
www.findhornpress.com

Contents

Dedication

I dedicate this book to the memory of my father and mother, and to my immediate biological family, Bill, Michele, and Jim, for their on-going contribution to my rich life and personal growth path.

I also dedicate this book to my spiritual family of soul sisters—Jennifer, my best friend and business guru; Sandie, my daily inspiration, treasured friend and creative mentor; Bess, who mirrors the best of spiritual growth to me at every turn; Joyce, who by her purity of spirit and commitment to personal work, guides me to my higher self in times of struggle and to my favorite human, my niece Anne, who said to her aunt one day, "You go, girl."

Acknowledgements

Authors are fond of saying that no book is ever the result of one person's input. I'd like to take that one stage further by adding that no life, dream, or creation is ever the result of one person's efforts. Thus, I'd like to acknowledge the following:

Gina Mazza Hillier for her magnificent writing, artful way with a word, ready laugh and investigative spiritual leanings; Sandie Sedgbeer for her inspired genius, editing prowess and willingness to go for the best; John Evanko for his brilliant mind, quick wit and open, willing spirit; Jennifer Evanko for her ground-breaking business savvy and elevated new thought perspectives; Findhorn Press for believing in the out-of-the-box nature of this book and me; Uran Snyder for her loving loyal, quiet and peace-filled nature; Gail Torr for her friendship, candor, lively British perspective and professional expertise; CosmiKids' funders, executives, directors, vibes and all-age members for their willingness to believe in the unseen and join me for the ride; Mallika Chopra and her Dad for their early-on support and endorsement; Deb Coyle for her unconditional love, friendship and belief in me; Cesar Zapata for his design genius and Colombian spirit; Abe Gurvin for his psychedelic designs, loving manner and tie-dyed persona; MeSue Anania and Jan Sixsmith for their continuing hometown support; Freya Christian for her conscious legal practices, delightful friendship and no-nonsense manner; Gary Szenderski for his wise guidance and truth (with a small 't'); Esther Dormer for her style, vision and grace, and last but by no means least, Karynne Boese for her unwavering integrity and willingness to take our conversations to the edge and beyond.

> "We acknowledge in others the radiance and
> majesty of the human condition within ourselves."

I offer this thought here in the knowledge that we are all one.

1.

Car Rides with My Father

"Let's get lost," my father would occasionally announce when I was eight or ten years old.

It was our favorite dad-daughter pastime. We'd take leisurely Sunday drives and lose our way on purpose. I couldn't foresee how precious that one-on-one time with my father would soon become any more than I could predict where we would end up on our mini road trips.

"Now, help me find our way back," Dad would say, and I'd do my best to retrace the maze of roads that appeared through the car window.

Eventually, we would reemerge onto familiar streets leading towards the city. As Pittsburgh's skyline appeared before us, Dad would remark about the bustle of activity that took place there during the week.

"You know, Judy, each one of those tall buildings, and the companies in them, were built on a single idea." My father seemed to know (even if I didn't yet understand myself) that I was a sponge for this sort of visionary thinking, so willing to absorb his lessons about business, big dreams and life in general.

I listened earnestly as he talked of Pittsburgh's heyday, when steel baron Andrew Carnegie forged US Steel Company, Henry Clay Frick created a coke dynasty and the Mellon family bankrolled them. Dad knew the industry inside and out. For many years, he worked as a sales representative for various steel companies, including US Steel.

My dad traveled a lot on business. And when he was in town, much of his time was spent solo; entertaining customers in restaurants, reading in his den or presiding over important grilling duties during our family barbecues. In retrospect, he was a man who enjoyed his solitude. I didn't have a lot of one-on-one with my dad, so when I did, I treasured every moment and held onto every word. When he gave of himself, he did so fully from his heart; it was as though I was the only thing on his mind at the time. I was like a bee to honey. I would snuggle up close, wrapped within his kind, patient focus, whenever I had the chance.

"And that impressive building is home to PPG Industries," he'd explain while on those car rides. "You know, glass making is a close second to steel here."

Dad once told me a story about the industrialist John D. Rockefeller, Sr., whose link to our general area in the 1800s was oil refining in the northwestern region of Pennsylvania. When Rockefeller was twelve (about the same age I was at the time), he saved $50 by raising turkeys and working for neighbors. His mother, who was a religious and disciplined woman, encouraged him to loan that $50 to a local farmer at seven percent interest payable in one year. When the farmer repaid the loan with interest, Rockefeller's passion for using money to serve the greater good was sparked. "He spent 40 years building Standard Oil into the world's largest company, which made him the world's richest man," Dad commented. "Then he spent his last 40 years giving it away for the benefit of others." Hearing this story about Rockefeller's life was the first time I began to ponder the idea that money, too, can be a form of love that we can share with others—and not something to be hoarded just for oneself. I learned years later in a magazine article that Rockefeller had a soft spot for children, always remembering to hand out nickels or dimes to them as he went about his important work.

As our Sunday jaunts took us nearer to the city, we couldn't miss the sprawling Heinz 57 factory along the Allegheny River, steam roiling up through its chimneys. "The factory workers are what make that company really tick," Dad would offer. "Each one is just as important as the executives who steer the operations." Was Dad trying to inspire me through his own experiences, or had he already intuited the early stirrings of my own philosophy? I suspect he knew that all I needed was a nudge.

As we cruised by, I imagined plastic-capped workers on the assembly line helping tens of thousands of ketchup bottles, baby food jars and vegetable soup cans make their way to tables across the world. Like every grade-schooler in Pittsburgh, I had a pickle-shaped pin with the number 57 in the middle, a testament to the marketing genius and whimsy of the Heinz organization.

"Always remember, Judy, you were born in a town of great success, great innovation, great wealth."

In the rearview mirror of my consciousness, I can see how values and dreams that are lovingly instilled in us at a tender age—especially by our parents—have lasting resonance. I have always believed in my heart that small ideas can lead to great things, and that finding one's own way is essential.

And I still wear my pickle pin.

My father had an entrepreneurial streak of his own. When I was in third grade, he purchased a company that was already a going concern, Goldsborough & Vansant. His company was doing well so that my mom, dad, older brother Bill, sister Michele and me moved into a bigger house on Rolling Hills Road, a beautiful brick home with white porch pillars in the manicured suburban neighborhood of Whitehall, Pennsylvania. The stone houses around us were inspired by French architecture—very modest by today's standards but, back then, I thought we'd plopped into the lap of luxury. I loved our home. Lazy days were spent sitting by the fireplace in the downstairs game room, reading Shakespeare (probably because that just happened to be on our bookshelves) and my favorite childhood book of all time, *Le Petit Prince* by Antoine de Saint-Exupéry. The essence of that novel, which is distilled in an eloquent line of dialogue by the fox, remains my personal mantra to this very day: *On ne voit bien qu'avec le cœur, l'essentiel est invisible pour les yeux.* "It is only with the heart that one can see rightly; what is essential is invisible to the eye." I also found it very cool that Saint-Exupéry's little prince was technically an extraterrestrial—a very smart one who waxes poetically about simple truths that many of us humans seem to forget as we grow older.

The corner chair in my father's comfy den was another favorite reading nook. Oddly, I really didn't enjoy reading at school, but at home, I was like the proverbial hungry bookworm, devouring everything within reach. Since Dad kept a fascinating collection of finance, business and self-improvement books in that space, I fed my mind and fueled my dreams of growing up to be a successful business person just like him; I read several times all of the great motivational classics in Dad's collection such as *Think and Grow Rich* by Napoleon Hill, *Art of War* by Sun Tzu, *How to Win Friends and Influence People* by Dale Carnegie and titles by management visionary Peter Drucker. While I may not have comprehended much from these serious writings as a child, I certainly appreciated them years later when I really began to develop my own new paradigm business philosophies.

On occasion when I was a young girl, Dad would bring me to his office at Goldsborough & Vansant. Mom would have me wear a well-matched outfit and patent leather shoes—not to impress but out of respect for my father's position. Dad dressed conservatively with buttoned-up, starched white shirts, polished wingtips and a Stetson dress hat. I felt important walking with him, hand in hand, down the company's hallways, my little shoes click-click-clicking on the marble floors. Through young eyes, I observed how he interacted with employees and other business people, and they with him. Always mild-mannered, with a kind, loving smile, I noticed that Dad treated the custodial workers the same way he treated the executive vice president of US Steel. That impression stays with me to this day and is, perhaps, a big reason why fairness is a driving force in my personal and work life. Maybe, subconsciously, I hope to live up to my father's inherent moral code, something that came quite naturally to him.

Because of Dad's professional stature, I grew up around country clubs and learned to play golf well—a hobby that I still enjoy. I didn't think of our family as being privileged. It was just the life we knew. Of course, I can see now that being raised in such an environment has afforded me a certain comfort level to "conduct business on the course," when necessary. But neither of my parents ever put on airs. They had class and brains, and what they valued most was kindness, personal honor and a solid work ethic.

I learned from watching my father that risk-taking is a natural and even enjoyable part of business. His love of golf led him to purchase and operate a miniature golf course for several years. It was my first exposure to what a friend of mine calls PLERK, the interspersion of play and work. (I believe to this day that work doesn't have to be just work, it can be also be easy, breezy and fun). My brothers, sister and I spent many hours on those mini-greens and became veritable putt-putt pros. A healthy sibling rivalry would sometimes rear its head. Make-shift playoffs and championships ensued. Pressure mounted. Score cards were thrown. Clubs were flung. Whenever things started to really get out of hand, the sight of Dad, ever patient, walking slowly towards us with a concerned look would snap us back to good-mannered reality.

Dad's creative nature and love of golf led him to invest in a newfangled innovation called the Golf-It machine—coin operated, interactive stations that were virtual golf holes where the player could stand on a platform, hold their favorite golf iron, view a photo of a famous golf hole, and take a swing at a ball that was connected to a metal post in the floor. The golf ball never went anywhere but, based on the force and accuracy of the player's swing, the machine would mirror its expected trajectory on a 10-foot screen. Dad was so proud of those machines—imagining, as inventors do, that they would be the Next Big Thing. I admired so much (and still do) that he allowed his adventurous side to take flight and took chances with something he loved. Through the lens of my own experiences as an entrepreneur, I can appreciate that he must have been saddened when that miniature golf course closed or when the invention he funded didn't take off as anticipated. I respect him even more now that I've had a taste of placing on the line one's time, money, personal resources and reputation—even enduring questioning and ridicule—to follow one's personal creation through to fruition. I felt bad for him at the time but the lesson I came away with was this: the joy derived from exploring the uncertain or unknown is just as valuable as the end result—especially when it involves one's passion. My father went on to love the game of golf after the dream of his invention was put to rest.

Dad's entrepreneurial flair rubbed off on me at a young age. My very first undertaking at the age of eight, I'm proud to say, was the most sought after and successful private-sector venture on the entire Rolling Hills Road block. Yes, Judy's Sweet Shoppe was a fine example of what's possible in a free-market economy that's devoid of the word "competition." My establishment was all about collaboration and empowerment. Kids would travel from houses away in the summer heat, even ride bikes and scooters up to the ridge where I lived, to align with our vision of a tastier world. The pay wasn't much but the perks were sweet.

With precocious accuracy, I was able to assess each kid's skills. Jerry liked art so we nurtured his budding talent by appointing him our chief cardboard sign maker. My crazy friend Lacey was a born saleswoman. She could sell the shell off a tortoise before it had time to consider homelessness. Lacey was a natural to head up merchandising. Painstakingly, we'd line up our precious inventory by flavor (all chocolates together), color and texture (makes for a beautiful display) or size on our card-table storefront along the sidewalk. When business was slow, Lacey wasn't shy about taking her elevator pitch down the street, even into backyards and alleyways. I admired her gumption and, I have to say, learned some valuable techniques by watching her in action.

My friend Sarah's braces forbade her from eating candy of all sorts; nonetheless, she became masterful at operations. At any given moment, she could provide a full run-down of how many red versus black licorice sticks we'd sold to date, and how many wax Coke bottles were in inventory. If sales were in a slump, my team and I would meet in the executive suite (a neighbor's tree house) and devise strategies to increase our market share. Bundling penny candy in creative packaging for five cents a piece worked like a charm. That alone upped our margins. With a signing bonus of a Snickers bar, we enlisted manpower from our local paperboy. Doing so enabled us to pull off a Sunday paper ad campaign: hand-crafted flyers with packets of Sweeties taped near a message that read: "This entitles recipient to one free cream-swirl lollipop or roll of butterscotch LifeSavers at our Rolling Hills retail location."

On balmy days, we took full advantage of neighborhood thirstiness by increasing production of Kool-Aid—and, on special occasions, fresh-squeezed lemonade. I wasn't blind to the fact that my colleagues were working under adverse conditions in the summer heat (I cared about their health and well being) so I didn't mind one bit cutting into profits by offering drinks on the house from noon on. (Mom didn't like us drinking sugary drinks before lunchtime.)

All in all, the Sweet Shoppe was a tremendous learning experience. Even on days when we were up to our eyeballs in Necco wafers with no clue how to unload them before school started in the fall, some miracle would occur (a boy's softball team would walk by our stand after a game, famished and thirsty) or we'd come up with a mutually satisfactory means to sell the remainder of our goods (offer it at a discount to a homebound neighbor for Halloween candy). Live and learn. Of course, we didn't realize we were engaged in an important rehearsal for the future back then; we were just a bunch of neighborhood kids playing at business and having fun.

⊸◈⊱

My father naturally encouraged me to go for whatever creative ideas I came up with, as well as face any fears that may have prevented me from doing so. In my innocence, I had typical little-girl fears, and Dad didn't discount that they were, for me, very real. I would sometimes become frightened, for example, when storms washed through our neighborhood. As I peered out the living room picture window at rainwater streaming down the road and gushing into the storm drains along the sidewalk, I would imagine our house being whisked away. Dad never said, "Judy, that's silly" or "Don't be ridiculous." His response was to take my hand, walk me outside in the middle of a rainstorm and show me that the storm drains on our road could more than handle the flow of water.

I was also terrified of our neighbor's dog, Tippy, a terrier mix. To this day, I can still picture Tippy in his little red coat as I walked the wooded path through this neighbor's yard on my way to school. I would shake in my blue-plaid boots whenever I saw him skipping around outside. One day, he barked and charged towards me. I screamed and ran home crying.

"That dog hates me!" I told my parents.

Dad set aside the newspaper he was reading. "Let's go see Tippy."

"What?" I asked in horror.

"Let's go."

Together, we walked over to the neighbor's yard (at least Dad walked, I kind of dragged). As we approached, I could feel my body begin to tense up, just as it had done so many times before, walking to school on my own. As if on cue, that darn Tippy appeared out of nowhere just as we approached and charged straight at me. Terrified, I jumped on the hood of a parked car and started to cry again.

"It's okay," Dad spoke softly. "Calm down, he's just a little dog, he won't hurt you. See?"

Catching my breath through my tears, I stood motionless for what seemed like a long time. Tippy ceased his yipping and stared up at us, tongue drooping left. After a few minutes, he became disinterested and walked away. Dad whisked his arm around me and carried me back to the house. This small incident took on greater meaning for me when I learned years later that my father was also afraid of dogs. He did that for me—he moved past his own fears to help me combat mine. Or, maybe we helped each other in some way.

Fear is a multifaceted concept. While there are things in life that we cannot change, I've come to realize that fear is simply a state of mind that can, for the most part, be controlled and directed. As the saying goes, FEAR is "false evidence appearing real." The subconscious mind stores memories and we "never forget" certain things that happen to us (that darn Tippy!) even though we may have to reach into the depths of our memory bank to retrieve them (I'd completely forgotten about the little yipper until I sat down to write this chapter).

Life is filled with risks, and one of the greatest risks we can face in life is allowing fear to shackle and restrict the full emergence of our talents. We all have awkward coming-of-age stories to tell that speak to the fear of what others might think of us. A small example that comes to mind when I reflect on my junior high school years is getting braces the week before cheerleading tryouts. (Isn't that how life happens sometimes?) Fearing ridicule from metal-mouth syndrome, I didn't want to try out. Mom sat with me at the kitchen table the night before and listened intently to my worries as Dad leaned on the counter, standing above me with his warm, supportive smile. Together, they talked me through my fears. With that encouragement from my parents, I not only made the squad but became captain in my senior year. As a result, I learned a thing or two in those formative years about leadership and teamwork.

In our teens, we are especially vulnerable to losing part of our true selves. I was sometimes called a "goody two shoes" in high school (and by my older brother and sister at home) possibly because I always had a smile on my face or never really got into any big trouble. I didn't do drugs, or skip school or plan pranks like some of my classmates, and I was proud of not going awry. I wasn't in any particular clique; I got along with the geeks, the jocks and the hoods (troublemakers). I fluttered around the periphery and made friends with a lot of people. I'm still that way, I think. I don't see anything wrong in getting along with anyone and everyone.

Not that I was an absolute angel. If anyone could have pushed me beyond my good girl reputation, it would have been my dear friend MeSue (full name: Marina Sue Bernadette Ann Martino). When I first laid eyes on MeSue, she was running down the sidewalk outside our junior high school trying to escape the fury of a science teacher as he ran after her, shaking his fist. The teacher finally caught up to her, gripped her by the elbow and led her back into the school. Dressed all in black with a twinkle in her eye, MeSue winked at me as she was escorted to the principal's office. I later learned what had fueled the teacher's wrath. MeSue had filled a hypodermic syringe with indelible ink and squirted it on him in the hallway.

Soon after, MeSue and I saw each other at a school dance, exchanged names and laughed about the hypodermic caper. Over the music blaring in the school gymnasium, we talked for hours and became fast friends.

Wiser and wilder, MeSue asked me to meet her at the railroad tracks near our neighborhood. Once there, she instructed me on the correct technique for inhaling cigarette smoke, and she and I both learned how to mix cola and aspirin for a fun feeling. MeSue had genuine sparkle and a knack for finding fun around every corner. In ninth grade, she egged me on to go with her to meet some guy in an abandoned church building who supposedly wanted to take our photographs for use at a modeling agency. I didn't feel good about this darkly dressed guy from the beginning, and couldn't understand why he had approached us for this modeling job. "Who's it for? And when?" I asked, suspiciously. Ignoring my questions, he crouched down on his haunches, looked around with a twitch to see who was watching, and then surreptitiously pulled out a used pair of panty hose from his pocket. Eeeww! I felt a funny knowing in my tummy that rose to my heart and out my mouth. "No, no we're not interested!" I said in a rush, as I dragged MeSue away with me.

So, when push came to shove, MeSue and I took care of each other and grew into honest-to-goodness blood sisters, even pricking our pointer fingers and pressing them together one evening in the summer of 1969. "Soul sisters forever," we vowed. Far from being a bad influence, MeSue was, and still is, a wonderful example of being bold and living life to the fullest. Even now, our friendship abounds with adventure and laughter. MeSue has completely remained who she has always been, and I admire her for that.

And I will always remember that MeSue was a shoulder to lean on when I needed it most during our junior year. Something was about to happen that would call up deep fears and vulnerabilities that I didn't even know I was capable of feeling. I was about to walk outside in the midst of an emotional rainstorm, only this time, my father wouldn't be there to hold my hand.

2.

Meeting Ernest Hemingway

The interesting thing about a crisis is how it insulates space and time. Hours surrounding it detach and separate in our memory. Earlier moments are redrawn within a tragic context. They become deceptive in their simplicity. Cereal poured in a bowl. Schoolbooks gathered on the table. Dishes placed in the sink.

Dad was readying one morning for a business trip to Warren, Ohio. Over a quick breakfast, I shared with him that our cheerleading squad was preparing for a competition that weekend. Dad always gave me his full attention when I had something important to say. And he understood me in a way that no one else could. I put my bowl in the sink and hugged him from behind, catching a whiff of Old Spice, which was his favorite everyday cologne. I flew out the door for school with a smile, glancing back at his handsome attire as he prepared to leave.

That glance is still etched in my mind.

Word came in the middle of the night. While crossing the street in downtown Warren, Dad had been hit by a taxi and killed instantly. He was 50, I was just 16.

To this day, I still remember being awakened in the middle of the night by the insistence of the front door bell. I sat up with a start, then immediately jumped out of bed and followed my mom downstairs, the haze of sleep still clouding my thoughts. Answering the door, she talked quietly through the locked screen with two uniformed police officers. I leaned over the polished wooden banister to listen more intently. I heard the words "automobile accident" and "hospital," then suddenly mom was rushing up the stairs past me to her dressing room. Peering down, I could see the two young men standing stiffly in our living room, their hats clasped respectfully in their hands. I followed mom up the stairs and quietly closed the door behind me as I entered her room. I watched as she fumbled through her closet looking for something to throw on.

"Did they say how dad is? Did they say what hospital he's in?" I asked with growing trepidation.

"Don't you know… don't you know?" She hissed in an almost angry yet strangely trance-like murmur.

"Know what?" I echoed softly.

"Don't you know the reason they're not telling us what hospital he's in?" She snapped.

I couldn't work out why mom seemed to be so angry at me, and yet so distant at the same time, as though preoccupied in some world of her own.

Turning her back to me and delving deeper into her closet so that she was almost hidden from sight, Mom blurted out: "They're not telling us because he's not in any hospital…

There was a pause. *"It's because he's dead!"* She screamed.

The words hit me like a punch in the solar plexus. I was literally knocked aside as Mom swung past me and hastened towards the stairs to rejoin the officers.

Through my numbness and shock, I heard one of the officers ask if there was anyone who could stay with me and my younger brother, Jim, who was upstairs in bed, still blissfully unaware of the tragedy that had befallen our family.

Suddenly, I wanted to run and hide. I wanted to dash upstairs and huddle beneath my warm covers and awaken later when the bad dream was over. I wanted to cry and scream and yell that it wasn't true, that my dad—my hero—would be coming home soon. But it wasn't a dream, and there was nowhere to go, and there was nothing to do but stay where I was, locked in the waking nightmare of my disbelief as the sadness and grief slowly turned me inside out, transforming me overnight from a normal happy teenager without a care in the world into an empty shell of a girl.

From that day forward, everything seemed to move in slow motion, exaggerating the emptiness I now felt. The following weeks and months passed in an agonizingly slow blur of extended family interactions, awkward social gatherings and endless whispered talk of the dead. I had never lost anyone close to me before. Grief was a foreign concept. I didn't know what to do with it. One minute my dad was there and the next, he wasn't. My grief went so deep my feelings got buried beneath a layer of numbness.

I drifted through each day in a daze. The songbirds seemed to have left the magnolia tree outside my bedroom window. I noticed, for the first time, the shadow it cast over the lawn. On reflex, I'd walk by Dad's upstairs office after dinner and knock on the door, forgetting he wasn't there. Unable to sleep, I'd pine for one more of our late-night snacks together—luncheon meats and cheeses piled high into "samiches," and tea with milk and sugar. As a sensitive middle child, I was forever trying to fix everything and make everyone else feel alright. Dad was the one who had always made *me* feel alright. With his passing, I was left on my own. I knew that my mother loved me dearly, but no one understood me on such a deep level as my Dad. He was my first true mentor, the first in a long line of teachers—painful and pleasant, inspiring and even devastating—all of whom gave me opportunities to challenge old concepts and become open to new ones. It was years before I was able to see that through his early passing, Dad had provided me with two bittersweet gifts that would profoundly shape me in the fullest sense: an overwhelming urge to understand the meaning of death and of life, and a deep yearning to honor him by creating something he would be proud of, and imbuing it with the very best and highest qualities he had demonstrated as a human being.

I began, unconsciously at first, to craft the framework of a very personal legacy from my father. Whether it was out of my desperate need to make sense of his sudden death or to assuage my overwhelming feelings of loss, I shall never know; but as the months passed, I slowly reconnected with myself. I decided that the best way to pay special tribute to my dad was to choose two of his best qualities, as impressed upon me throughout his life, and endeavor to live them in my own life. That way, he'd live on through me. Through my actions, his essence would remain. I chose his kind-hearted ways and sense of adventure.

Dad was gone but somehow life went on. I followed in my older sister's footsteps upon high school graduation and left for college to major in sociology. I worked a variety of jobs in the days following my graduation from Denison University—cocktail waitress, car salesperson, gas station merchandising rep, advertising agency receptionist and part-time hostess—and each one taught me something valuable. Back then, I was happiest as a cocktail waitress. I enjoyed the night life, the people I worked for and the money. I knew on some level that I was good with people of all ages and backgrounds, and that I could "read" people's needs and personality types quite well. I frequently received big tips that surprised even me. After that, I worked in different venues for a variety of personality types. My sensitive nature was bruised on many occasions with hot-tempered bosses and fear-based managers. I discovered that I thrived in independent work structures where the staff were empowered, not demeaned, and positively supported, not reprimanded.

After Dad had died, my older brother Bill had immediately stepped up to the plate and taken over Dad's company, Goldsborough & Vansant. I was amazed and impressed by my brother's ability to rise to the occasion, step into dad's shoes and very quickly master the intricacies of running a business that he knew absolutely nothing about. I often wondered if Bill liked what he did, or if, as the oldest surviving male, he had simply felt an awkward responsibility to the family for the welfare of our dad's business. I was intrigued by this because Bill and my dad had never seemed to see eye-to-eye. On the contrary, many were the occasions when their arguments had erupted into violent outbursts or ended with someone stomping out of the house, slamming the door behind them. Yet Bill didn't flinch from stepping into my father's shoes and facing his spirit on a daily basis as he took over the running of his company. I often wonder what that must have been like for my brother. Did he come to know my dad through osmosis and in some way learn to understand him better through the work that he did? Or did my dad perhaps lend a helping advisory hand from spirit as he guided my brother from above?

Some years later, I too went to work for Goldsborough & Vansant. I thought it would be interesting to work in the family business, and perhaps get to know my big brother a little better, as he and I had become estranged in my adolescence. I never understood the growing chasm between us, as I was just a youngster when, for some inexplicable and to this day unspoken reason, Bill pulled away from me emotionally. I also decided to join the family business after becoming disillusioned by the time I spent at my former job at an ad agency. The people there were mean and ego-centered and too busy to connect on any real level. I thought by going to work at the company that my father had begun, I might be able to reconnect to those feelings of kind-heartedness and adventure. Sadly, that was not the case. Throughout the five years I worked at the family business, I never really felt a part of the culture or mindset. What I did feel was disengaged and under-challenged. I was filled with a yearning to find a place to work that felt good. By then, the economic atmosphere in Pittsburgh had markedly shifted. The coke, coal and steel industries that had made Pittsburgh great were now on the decline. Plants were being shut down, boarded up and left to rust. Production at US Steel plummeted 100 percent and the company founded by Pittsburgh native Andrew Carnegie, one of the most successful philanthropists and captains of industry in the history of the United States, dropped its name and became USX. Young people were making an exodus from the city's workforce. I considered doing the same. I had my friends from high school and college, but I was becoming weary of the vacuous nature of the after-work happy hours and the 20-something pop culture. I was seeking substance and I had no idea where to begin looking for it.

Then I met an amazing man named David at a black tie party given by one of my neighbors. From the moment I first met him, I felt a strong affinity with him, a sense that I *knew* him somehow. Tall, dark and handsome and ten or so years older than me, David's quietly sophisticated style really appealed to me. He spoke softly and kindly, yet I sensed a deep sadness about him. We ended up talking for hours, during which time he confided that he was in the midst of post-divorce visitation negotiations. I was completely taken by his gentle demeanor and underlying kindness, which became apparent to me on an energetic level almost immediately. I went to sleep that night floating on a cloud. I distinctly remember waking up with a start at three in the morning, my heart filled with glee. I was up and wide awake as the young school children made their way to school, guided by the crossing guard at the street intersection below the French window of my studio apartment. I sat perched on the window ledge in my nightgown, exchanging pleasantries with the crossing guard below. It was like that scene out of *West Side Story* when Maria wakes up full of the joys of spring the morning after meeting Tony. The birds sang so gloriously that day. Everything looked brighter and I felt my heart strings resonating in a way that I had never felt before. I didn't know when, but I knew that David and I would be together again soon. I couldn't wait to spend more time with him and get to know him better.

The following day, he sent me flowers and champagne with a thank you note for listening so attentively. When I called to thank him, he invited me to dinner.

As we drove together in his car, he asked, "Would you like to go into the city or should we fly to Paris?"

"Are you serious?" I responded.

"Yes, whatever you prefer," he remarked casually.

I nearly fell off the passenger's seat of his midnight blue town car when he turned the steering wheel and started heading towards the airport freeway.

"We can hop a plane immediately," he said. "We're headed in the right direction."

He WAS serious—not in an egocentric, flashy way but with a frolicsome spirit. I was taken with David from the start. He was singing my song.

All the same, since I hardly knew him, I felt it best to opt for a local restaurant. As I stated my desire to go somewhere close by, he smiled quietly and turned the car around towards the city. That night will forever be emblazoned on my heart. We went to The Colony, a grand, Old World steakhouse with white-gloved waiters, soft lighting and romantic music wafting through the rooms. We talked about business, investing and our likes and dislikes. Beyond our conversation, I felt the essence of David's inner self, which completely turned me on. He was smart, witty and quietly observant. For the first time in my life I fell deeply in love.

For the next three months, I lived a fairy tale with my knight in shining armor. On surprise out-of-town trips, we'd walk amidst the fragrant cherry blossoms in Washington, DC, lose ourselves in long, lazy afternoons of lovemaking, and awake to flower petals on our pillows and birds singing on the hotel veranda. Then we'd dress in our finery and dine on French cuisine and champagne. Everything was at once brighter in my world. Colors became richer, smells more vivid and my heart opened to the promise of time spent with someone who matched my every desire.

David was successful, worldly and knowledgeable about investments, something that has always piqued my interest. I'd always had a thirst for learning and an appetite for business—characteristics that my dad had both personified and encouraged in me. With David, I felt that I'd found someone who matched my dreams of grandeur, adventure and passion so, of course, I believed that he was the man for me. Interestingly enough, he was in the steel business, just like my father and brother, and so I looked up to him in the same way that I had looked up to these other significant males in my life.

Another factor that attracted me to him was his love for children, and most especially his own daughter. At one point, during a trip we made together to Washington, D.C. we met up with some friends of his who had a young daughter. I was mesmerized by David's capacity to relate to the young girl and spend time, hunkered down so that he could be eye level with her, engaged in a serious discussion that encompassed dolls, the art of twirling and party dresses. He was child-like, sensitive and kind—and that spoke volumes to me.

Then, out of the blue, all my dreams came crashing down around me.

Suddenly, David became frightened by the intensity of our relationship and sought to end it. At one point, he completely disappeared for four days. I was frantic with worry. When he surfaced, he explained that he'd been out of commission for a while and wanted to clear his mind. I knew he was still enmeshed in a problematic situation with his former wife, and I tried my best to understand and be accepting of that. But it wasn't enough.

Our relationship had become more serious than David wanted or could handle at the time. He didn't come right out and say that it was over. He simply never called again.

Losing David was the last thing I had envisioned or wanted. The contrast between the David I had lived, loved, laughed and dreamed with for the past three months and the David who was now so abruptly cutting me out of his life was too great for me to get my head around. Over and over again I asked myself: *What did I do wrong?*

To say the least, I was devastated. I had loved David with all of the passion and fervor of a 27-year-old experiencing her first real grown up love, and I mourned his loss with all the anguish and grief of someone who had not yet come to terms with the sudden death of her father. Looking back, perhaps I was simply in love with the dream of someone like David; the fantasy of knowing that there's something more out there—passion and a soul-level connection with a man who appreciates the finer things—living large, being completely in love with life, and basking in the certainty that anything is possible. I wanted my life to be like that. The single lifestyle no longer fit me. All I yearned for was a life of meaning, substance and union with a like-minded other. In those twelve short weeks with David I had discovered heaven. Coming on the heels of such bliss, the abrupt and sudden plunge into hell cracked my heart wide open. It was the agony and the ecstasy all rolled into one and my young, naïve sensibilities just couldn't handle the high voltage input.

David and I never did travel to Paris but the impact of our whirlwind romance hastened a profound inward journey that I would begin exactly one week after our breakup. This trip would send me to another world entirely, and returning from it would be a testing fire for how to live the rest of my life.

Funny, how crises insulate events in space and time. Wine poured in a glass . . . a classic novel sitting on the bar . . . a walk down familiar cobblestone streets...

To be close to my nine-to-five job at my brother's company, I had taken my very first studio apartment atop Mt. Washington, which offers glorious views and breathtaking vistas of the "city of a thousand bridges." A childhood friend of mine, Frank, owned a wonderful Italian restaurant in the city called Piccolo Piccolo. One day after work, I stopped by the City Club to exercise then went by Frank's place. As I approached the bar, Frank could immediately see the despair, grief and incomprehension written all over me.

"What on earth happened to you?" he said as he sat me down and poured me a glass of his best cabernet. Tears flowed copiously as I hiccupped my way through the abrupt and devastating end of my relationship with David.

Just then, an older gentleman walked into the restaurant. My eyes were immediately drawn to him. He had what looked like a light around him, a warm glow. I didn't understand at the time that I was seeing his aura, or energy field, and that he was the equivalent of what I would now call a light being. All I knew was that there was something so different about him that his appearance had immediately cut through the fog of my misery. I couldn't take my eyes off him.

He walked over and sat down at a table next to the window, quiet and unassuming, and began to read a newspaper. The sound of Frank's voice snapped me back to the present moment.

"Hey, that guy doesn't have a tie on." Frank ran a dignified, upscale establishment—which included a dress code.

"Frank, I don't care what you do, but that man is a very special man," I said without even knowing why I'd said it. "There's something about him. I don't know what it is but please be kind to him," I asked, almost pleadingly. "Doesn't he look like Ernest Hemingway?"

"Yea, he kind of does," Frank concurred.

Before Frank could do anything, the man left quietly then returned a short while later wearing a tie. As the tears continued to drip slowly down my face, I sipped my wine, stealing glances every so often in Hemingway's direction. Then he got up to leave. Strangely, I felt a nudge of sadness as he glided out the door, seemingly on air. It rendered me silent and I sat alone for a while in deep, far-away thought.

Next thing I knew, I glanced over my right shoulder and realized that another man was now seated at the bar stool next to me, reading a book. As our eyes connected, he closed the book and laid it on the bar. I blinked hard, disbelieving what I saw. It was a dog-eared copy of Hemingway's classic *The Old Man and the Sea*.

"So, you met my friend?" he said, matter-of-factly, but with an oddly mesmerizing undertone.

"Uh . . . uh . . . yea." I didn't know what to say.

 "Would you like to know more about him?"

"I guess," I responded, a bit dazed.

The man began to tell me about his very special friend. He called him Mr. Higgins.

"When Mr. Higgins travels, which he does quite frequently, not everyone notices him," the man explained. "He keeps mainly to himself. Those who do notice him are usually meant to meet him."

I stared at the man's hands as he spoke. They seemed oddly youthful compared to his face and age. His long, square fingernails had a backlit quality. His cuticles looked airbrushed.

"Mr. Higgins is staying at the Hilton. Would you like to meet him?"

"I'd love to," I said, still dazed, and not sure why I was having anything to do with these mysterious characters.

Oddly enough, I felt in my gut that he meant no harm. I said goodbye to Frank, and the man and I walked together through Market Square, a lovely cobblestone area in the middle of the city where people gathered to eat lunch, enjoy free concerts and stage civic rallies. In those days, other twenty-something's like me engaged in an activity we called M-Squared, where patrons of the bars and clubs in the square would spill out into the streets to continue their revelry. As we passed by a small crowd of people laughing and dancing in the night air, I felt a little like Alice in Wonderland traveling down the rabbit hole, yet I was falling with full consciousness. My logical mind was screaming "WHAT ARE YOU DOING?" but I knew, I just knew, that I was safe and protected. Finally, we arrived at the Hilton Hotel and walked into the lounge area.

"You wait here, I'll go and see if Mr. Higgins can meet with you now," the man instructed.

A length of time passed—several hours, perhaps—and the man still hadn't returned to the lounge. Disappointed, I realized that I wasn't going to meet Mr. Higgins a.k.a. Ernest Hemingway. By now it was past dark and I didn't want to walk all the way back to the parking garage by myself. What's more, I was immersed in this newfound energy field that was curiously alluring and intoxicating, far beyond the warmth I felt from the wine I'd drunk at Frank's place. It had started the instant I softly locked eyes with Mr. Higgins at the bar. Intuitively, I knew I was in the midst of something unlike anything I had ever experienced before, and that whatever it was would change my view of reality forever. At the time, I couldn't explain what was happening but I was certain that I wanted to continue down that rabbit hole for as long as I could. It was worth the risk. Nothing else mattered. My day-to-day concerns melted into the background, giving way to a brighter, higher-frequency dimension to life, as compared to how I'd always known it. I much preferred the new, quickened and more vibrant look and feel of this utopia and didn't want to break the spell. My instincts still confirmed that I was in no danger. With eyes wide open, I got a room at the hotel. Maybe I'd run into the two gentlemen the next morning. I reasoned that if I could speak to these men, they would help me make sense of the evening's surreal events.

The next morning, I awoke to find myself in another reality altogether. It was as if I had been sprung from a womb into a brand new, sensual world. I was overcome with a slowly building rush of gratitude, joy and unbounded love. Handel's *Water Music* was playing on the radio. I wept at the sound of it, which I heard not only with my ears but also through my heart, nose, eyes and skin. A sweet aroma of roses that had not been there before filled the room. Quietly and delightedly, I swam in the magic and mystery of those post-dawn hours, as the sunlight began to stream in through the windows. I didn't know how or why this was happening but I knew it was for me. This new reality I was experiencing felt strangely familiar.

I decided to order room service. Suitably, my bellman's name was Adam. Kind-hearted and soft spoken, he lifted the silver lid to reveal the first breakfast of the rest of my life. The eggs glistened with joy. I savored every bite. The enjoyment factor of everything took on a deep and richly textured proportion. I didn't want this bubble of bliss to pop. I felt grateful to be alive and knew somehow that what had occurred the night before had something to do with it—even though nothing had really happened.

The only thing that could draw me out of the nirvana of that hotel room was the possibility of seeing Mr. Higgins and his companion in the lobby. But they were nowhere in sight. Sensing they were gone, I checked out of the hotel.

And, for a few days afterward—according to my family and friends, at least—I checked out of my mind entirely.

3.

Judy Flew Over the Cuckoo's Nest

For the next few days, I wandered about in a glittery paradise. The very air had spark and dazzle. It shimmered as I walked. Instinctively, I found my way back to my apartment on Mt. Washington. Nothing looked the same. The streets and buildings were brighter. People's faces seemed softer, younger looking, refreshed. I knocked on the door of my first-floor neighbor, who was busy ironing. I kept Dana company while she starched and pressed a white blouse. I shared a few things about the past 24 hours. She gave me a questioning look.

"What planet are you from?" she chided. "Forget all that. Come with me into town. I'm meeting some friends."

I put a lid on my outlandish recounting of events and hopped in the car with Dana. Ironically, we ended up in Market Square, the same part of the city where I'd strolled with Mr. Higgins' friend. As we arrived at a familiar club, I was amazed that the stairs I'd climbed dozens of times now seemed different somehow. As we reached the third floor outdoor patio, I noticed a handful of acquaintances who had also taken on an odd appearance. Surrounding many of them were colored arcs of light—some clear, some bright, some with a murky, foreboding hue. *That's wild,* I thought. Then I heard a strange clatter in my mind—my voice but not my words—representing the thoughts of those around me. I also sensed things about these individuals from the colors that surrounded them. I could tell one woman was sickly, one guy felt troubled, and another gal was saying and doing two different things. I wanted to share this with someone but who would understand? Hell, even I couldn't completely fathom what was going on. How could I explain it to someone else?

After a while, as I left the club and walked the streets alone, I noticed "beings" that no one else seemed to see. These "people" were benevolent and helpful. I could talk to them. As thoughts formed in my mind, they would reveal themselves to me through a headline at a magazine stand, an overheard word from a passerby or a seeming response from a flower or tree. I observed myself being in this kaleidoscopic world of unexplainable events and rationalized that I must have died and gone to heaven. Honestly, I considered the possibility that some part of myself—my spirit or soul—had left my body and that I was experiencing this "human" world somewhere else. I was happily entranced in this new reality yet had no one to share it with. Forget about corroboration—I just wanted someone to pal around with in my new wonder zone.

It felt as though I had this little secret that I couldn't explain to anyone. I couldn't find words for it. I got the sense that the people around me, going about their business in the city, had no idea about this larger picture of things; of the true meaning behind our lives and what we do. They seemed like mice in a maze and I felt so grateful knowing there was some larger purpose behind it all. It was as if I was above myself and the events going on around me, looking down on them, appreciating this experience called life for the "play" that it was; aware that everyone had their part in this performance. I loved this new fantasy-type experience, the tingly, otherworldly feeling and the empowered sense of being. It felt oddly invigorating and even liberating, like I was exploring some strange new land. I felt like a visitor to a far-away planet, attempting to adjust to breathing new air and walking amidst laws of gravity that were completely foreign to me. I was seeing and sensing things that only a day before had been nonexistent in my life. Was I experiencing some great energy shift? Or had I somehow slipped into another dimension? I just didn't know. All I knew was that I liked this other reality; it spoke to something deep within me. I had no frame of reference for it, yet I knew it was something very special.

I'm not sure whether it was the intensity of the situation, my inability to integrate within my own system the heightened energies of my new reality, or my circuits slowly becoming fried, but as time passed I started to lose grip on what was real and what was part of my new-found fantasy world.

As I walked alone on a downtown street a few days later, a police car cruised to a halt beside me. Unable to provide any intelligible explanation, the policeman took me to the county jailhouse and locked me in a holding cell overnight. Still feeling as though I had fallen down a rabbit hole and unable to make anyone understand me, or the experience I was having, I decided that the best thing to do was to stop answering questions; it only seemed to be getting me deeper into trouble.

I lay on a dingy cot facing the cement wall, with nothing to do but wonder how all this had happened to me, and why. How had I managed to slip between the cracks into this new and curious reality? For some strange reason, I kept getting that it had something to do with my heart and how broken open it was. I started to piece together that it might also have had something to do with my noticing Mr. Higgins and the extra-sensory abilities that had suddenly started to surface. I wondered what it would be like to remain in this in-between netherworld, and never again find a foothold in either reality. Thinking that it would be so lonely to never again have someone to relate to, I began to cry.

Dear God, please lead me down the path of your choosing. I simply don't know anything anymore. I prayed, as I drifted into sleep.

The following morning I awoke to see the words "Judy was here" scribbled on the wall just ten inches from my astonished eyes. Breathing a sigh of relief, I took it to be a sign from God that I *Harness the power of prayer.* would be freed soon and that a better path would be opening up before me. Sure enough, a few hours later I was informed that I could leave. My mind was still foggy, and I didn't know what was going to happen next, but I was elated to be out in the sunlight again. I was driven home to my mother's house in a police car. What timing . . . It was Mother's Day.

Essentially, I'd been missing for several days. My mother had become worried after not hearing from me, as we usually talked daily. I was a bit unclear in my speech—not how my family was used to hearing me talk and behave. I attempted to tell Mom and my younger brother what had happened. Having learned from the previous night's experience that I needed to be careful about how much I revealed of what had been happening to me, I at first tried to be a little more careful about how I couched things. But obviously I wasn't careful enough. For sure, there was some kind of split going on in my consciousness. I was now occupying two realities—one was firmly rooted in the third dimension, the other seemed to be more holographic and expansive. While I quite liked it, I was having a hard time reconciling these different realities. From my perspective, I just needed to learn how to dwell effectively in both at the same time. From my family's perspective, something very worrying was going on. Not surprisingly, their reaction was one of discomfort and grave concern.

I can understand now why everyone thought I had lost my marbles. Once the dam of my reticence broke, I started telling them I knew the answers to all the world's mysteries. I rhapsodized about the meaning of love and the importance of forgiveness. I demonstrated my ability to read people's minds and it freaked them out. Overnight, it seemed the Judy they knew and loved had mysteriously turned into some kind of evangelist. I couldn't stop gushing love and trying to convince everyone about the beauty of life. A portal had opened up between me and the Divine and, what's more, I had no desire to close it. Lovers embracing on the sidewalk became a glorious depiction of spiritual love. People partying became a celebration of life and our experience of humanness. Conversations with cosmic beings became commonplace for me alone. Homeless people became enlightened souls. During my "episode," as it was later labeled by my family and healthcare professionals, I remember passing a homeless man on the sidewalk. When our eyes met, I was awash with a warm rush of good feelings and reverence for him. It was as though I was able to witness him as he authentically played his part in the scheme of our life on earth. I saw myself in him, and he in me. We were one, acknowledging each other lovingly on our separate yet co-mingled paths. It was as if I had suddenly been given the keys to understanding life, love, the universe . . . *everything!* Of course, it was impossible to convey any of this and not sound loony.

"Judy, you're not speaking or behaving normally," my mom pleaded. "You cannot be out and about telling people these kinds of things. You need to be hospitalized."

Frustrated and at my wit's end, I eventually gave in; partly because I was so exhausted I no longer had the will or strength to fight them. I had so cherished those past few days and was deeply saddened that it may all be coming to an end, not the least because no one in my life at that time could comprehend anything of which I spoke, nor ever would. So, certain that they knew what was best for me and glad of the chance to rest I agreed to voluntary committal.

Within 48 hours, I was admitted to the psychiatric ward of Jefferson Hospital. For backup, my mother called an older cousin to join us on the car ride to the hospital. As I stared out the window, I saw people gathered for a celebration with balloons and presents. I remember thinking that their gala symbolized the ongoing celebration of my becoming more of who I was meant to be, albeit through a method that was well beyond my comprehension. Yet, somewhere deep inside me, I felt a sense of inner joy and peace that all was just as it should be.

From this enlightened perspective, being checked into a mental hospital was a startling contrast.

I really had none of the awkward feelings one might expect about committing oneself to a mental hospital. I guess by that point I had been through so much that one more rung on the ladder didn't really seem to matter. On the one hand, I somehow intuited that I would be better for this experience. On the other, my reality check had become so outmoded that I no longer had any real barometer of measurement. So I simply went with the flow.

As I settled into my temporary home on the seventh floor ward and wandered about, I felt an odd, familiar kinship with the other patients, regardless of their ages. If there was one thing I could rely on here, it was the unspoken bond that existed among us. No one judged anyone. There were no condescending looks, and no questioning either. We simply met each other at whatever level we cared to come together. Some were heavily medicated. Some were clear and thoughtful. Others were so emotionally anesthetized it was difficult to reach them. I just shined on, in my own way, blissfully aware that I was being taken care of on a higher level.

The get-to-know-you interview with my assigned doctor comprised the usual list of mundane questions.

"What are your hobbies?" He asked, looking over his reading glasses, as if expecting to hear something outlandish.

Thinking back to springtime on the jogging trail, I smiled reflectively and said, "I love to run."

Crossing his legs, he removed his spectacles and, tapping the ear piece against his teeth, said, "Have you ever thought about what you're running from, Judy?"

Silence filled the room.

"Uh, no, but I can put some time into thinking about it, if you feel it may be important." I offered respectfully.

He continued to look at me, expressionless, for a few more minutes. Thinking he may be looking for another response, I thought a little harder.

"No," I concluded after several more seconds. "I just like to run. It feels good and it's healthy for both my mind and my body."

I didn't know what he made of my answer, and I didn't really care. I knew I wasn't mentally ill. In fact, when I walked into that hospital, although physically and emotionally weary, I was more fully conscious than at any other time in my life. But then, without giving me any reason, they put me on an antipsychotic medication that clouded my mind, and caused me to slobber and walk on my toes. It was a horrible experience, particularly coming so close on the heels of one that had left me feeling exquisitely clear, alive and more aware than I had ever been before. In spite of being drugged, however, and even though I went through periods of intense frustration and inner turmoil, both my sanity and innovative tendencies were still intact. After a few days, I started pretending to swallow the meds they kept giving me, and instead hid the pills under my tongue, a la Jack Nicholson in *One Flew Over the Cuckoo's Nest*.

Looking back on that experience of being drugged in a hospital, I now question how many other people out there in psychiatric wards across the country are really having spiritual awakenings, and how might we handle these crises differently based on our heightened understanding of human consciousness. I think about the millions of children and adults on Ritalin, Prozac and anti-depressants. What are we drugging them for—to suppress valid emotions or mini-spiritual awakenings? In some cases, the medication is necessary, especially if an individual might be of harm to themselves or others. In other cases, I often wonder whether we're medicating people simply because we don't know how otherwise to handle what's happening with them. Statistics show, for example, that spending time conversing with a mental patient does them as much if not more good than dosing them with meds. Perhaps we would all be better off if more of us were encouraged to "lose our minds". Maybe then we'd spend more time thinking from our hearts and acting from our souls.

I remember an especially poignant moment during my stay at Jefferson. Every month, the hospital social committee would coordinate a visit to a neighborhood theatre for movie time. We'd all pile into the big blue bus with "Jefferson Hospital" stenciled in oversized letters on the side. As the mind-numbing effects of my meds began to wear off, I started to act more like the old Judy, with a quicker wit and desire to get on with life "on the outside". So as the days wore on, I began to feel more and more misplaced, under constant watch and being labeled as sick when I knew I was anything but. So it was all the more wonderful when, on the day of our theatre trip the female bus driver, who was about the same age as me, suddenly looked me square in the eye at the end of a conversation we'd been having about movies, fashion and pop culture, and pronounced, "Girl, you don't belong here, do you?"

"No," I responded, "but it's okay. I'll be out soon and believe it or not, in many ways I've learned a lot from this experience."

She smiled and pulled the oversized lever to open the bus door. We emptied out onto Carson Street in front of the theatre. On the marquee was a teaser about our chosen movie, a story of "a misunderstood girl who comes of age and finds her true self." Even though I've long forgotten the film's title, its meaning remains with me. I felt as though that movie had been written, cast and directed solely for my benefit, and I left the theatre that day feeling divinely supported and loved. The truth of my situation was that I was confined imprisoned on a psychiatric ward, where many people feel belittled, worthless, hopeless, and suicidal. Yet at that moment, I felt blessed and thankful to be alive.

To keep myself occupied while in the hospital, I read whatever I could get my hands on and did my best to maintain some semblance of an exercise regime. One day during my stay, I saw a newspaper headline that stopped me in my tracks:

"Hemingway comes to Civic Arena."

The article reported on a convention taking place that weekend dedicated to the life and works of the Pulitzer and Nobel Prize winning author. Right away, logic kicked in and I reasoned away my experiences at Piccolo Piccolo and the Hilton as a Hemingway look-alike contest or some other coincidence related to the convention. If so, my Mr. Higgins would have won hands down. He was spot-on Papa. But that didn't explain the otherworldly quality of those two men—the glowing aura, the backlit fingernails and, most mysteriously, the feeling that came over me while in their presence. Maybe the deceased author was returning in spirit to check out his namesake expo, I considered, kind of like film directors do before they move into a city to begin production of a movie. In the end, I concluded that I was being given confirmation that what happened to me was real, as real as Hemingway's protagonist Santiago in *The Old Man and the Sea*, who wrestles against something greater than himself. We all face situations that define our lives. For Santiago, it was his struggle to haul in a great marlin, the biggest fish he'd ever seen. For me, my mystical experience was equally huge and unprecedented. Why Ernest Hemingway? I really don't know, but the man's name, Mr. Higgins, took on new meaning for me years later. Mr. Higgins, hmmm, Henry Higgins was the man who transformed Audrey Hepburn's character into the ravishing, cultured female in *My Fair Lady.* She became her higher self, in some respects. I was more akin to Eliza Doolittle, a common girl selling flowers in Covent Garden, than the fierce old fisherman. And my encounter with Mr. Higgins, though brief, was also powerfully transformational. So much so, that nothing in my life was ever the same.

What stayed with me most deeply from my episode is that there truly is a larger, grander plan in force that is guided by the Divine, and that the only thing that is important is love. In fact, it was the power of love (and having my heart cracked open with the sheer force of it) that had catapulted me into another reality. My experience had strengthened within me the belief that if we lead with love, then all will work out precisely as it should for all concerned. By the time I was discharged from the hospital two weeks later, I had made a commitment to becoming the best me that I could be. I knew my heart was in the right place. I vowed to continue keeping kindness and love as my guideposts and see where this took me. If we could all live from this higher space, well, to quote Eliza Doolittle, "Wouldn't it be loverly?"

I moved back to my mom's house after my hospital discharge and was obligated to weekly visits with an assigned psychiatrist, who turned out to be the same doctor whose care I had been under at the hospital. The poor man just didn't know what to make of me. Since I was out of confinement and able to speak more freely about my episode, I felt a little safer to divulge a bit more of the events leading up to my hospitalization. As I did so, his eyes grew wide. He'd shake his head and write lengthy notes on a pad that he kept close to his chest. I tried to be as honest as I could without being pegged a total kook. I wasn't sure about his seniority with the hospital and if he had the authority to throw me back into the blue bus, drugged and labeled beyond hope. So again, for the sake of survival, I started editing myself by not revealing everything that had happened to me.

This only seemed to annoy the psychiatrist more. I often felt that I couldn't win with him. When I clammed up, he got irritated. Yet when I told him the truth, he seemed to get really angry with me.

I remember the day when, out the blue, he suddenly announced that he was stopping our treatment sessions. Mom was with me that day. I had just been telling him the story about meeting Ernest Hemmingway. Somewhere in between my account of *The Old Man and The Sea* and being able to see auras and read minds, he threw his pencil down on the yellow pad of paper atop his crossed legs then turned to my mother and announced, "Your daughter is a schizophrenic, Mrs. Julin!"

On a deeper level, I think my mom must have understood that what was happening to me was a sort of spiritual door swinging open, because she immediately jumped to my defense.

"No she's not. She's fine!" She firmly declared.

"Well, if you don't accept my diagnosis there's nothing more I can do with her," the psychiatrist angrily pronounced. "Our sessions will have to end."

"There's nothing clinically wrong with my daughter," Mom insisted.

In a strange twist of fate, I ran (literally) into that same psychiatrist about a year later on the running trail at nearby Schenley Park. I jogged up right beside him, just to be friendly and acknowledge him, jogger to jogger. When he recognized me, he did a funny little double take and then took off like a speeding bullet. I couldn't believe it—a grown man, a professional mental healthcare worker, running away from someone who just wanted to reconnect and show him how normal she was after all. I shrugged my shoulders and took the higher trail that lay ahead. Then a thought struck me. It was too delicious to pass up. Turning around, I called after him: *"So what are YOU running away from, Dr. Richards?"*

On the surface, life once again returned to normal. But as I attempted to go on as usual, it was challenging for me to integrate what I was now seeing, feeling and witnessing with my daily reality. As the months went by and this heightened state gradually wore off, I mourned the loss of that feeling and yearned to get back to that higher realm. I began to read avidly on topics related to cybernetics, altered realities, expanded states of consciousness, spiritual practices, alien and other-planetary life, psychic experiences and the power of the mind in an effort to answer the two questions that now dangled over my days and nights: *What exactly happened to me? And why?* As I began to search internally for answers, I explored what had occurred immediately beforehand. I'd had a sublime whirlwind romance with David which had propelled me to new heights of love. His sudden decision to end our relationship had hurled me to the depths. My tender heart—fully exposed and then so abruptly shattered into pieces—seemed to invite this profound spiritual experience, which had lifted me from the depths and sent me to unimaginable heights far beyond love with another human being. This was communion with the Source, a state of being in love not with a person but with God, life, everything and everyone. And the absolute knowingness that we truly are all One.

As I've grown older, for some reason, I seem to have managed to retain the wonder and innocence of my childhood years—perhaps it is why I connect so well with children and, moreover, the reason for my chosen career path. There is something very special about the characteristics of children that call us to examine and dwell more deeply within our rich inner lives. We cannot squelch that magical realm, those wild and fantastic imaginings of our youth, for in them lie divine truths and a connection to the vast unknown that surrounds us. Children see and feel this naturally. I suspected from a very early age that this connection, forged from pure love, is available to all of us directly. It's one of those simple truths that Saint-Exupéry's little prince noticed that we humans seem to forget as we grow up.

Maybe because of the way I was raised, or perhaps because it's just part of my make-up, I've always felt drawn to goodness in others and I strived to be good, as well. When I was very young, this came naturally; I simply loved everybody. And I certainly didn't see anything wrong in wanting everyone else to love me. But as a teenager, I was sometimes ridiculed for these same qualities. Even my brother Bill once said to my mom, "Judy's just too nice. Get real. NOBODY is that nice."

I now believe the experience of expanded consciousness that I had in 1981 was a reward for keeping my heart and mind open to the power of kindness. It showed me another way to live that was more in accordance with my true nature, one guided by optimism and an internal calm. To this day—although life lessons have shown me that the world isn't always compassionate,—I strive to lead with love in everything: my thoughts, words, actions and interactions. I don't always get it right, and yes, sometimes I even fail miserably, but what I have learned is that the pendulum swings, and I do my best to accept all of my states of being with as much grace as I am capable of. To me, that's holding to a higher truth—my own truth. I believe it works for me.

After taking several months of R & R to reacquaint myself with life after psychotropic drugs, I returned to my normal routine of working in my brother's office from nine to five. Being there seemed oppressive because there was little room for free thinkers who were loving, creative and open to new ideas. I couldn't blame the people who entered into this work environment. It appeared that they were okay with their lot in life, although complaints, gossip and short tempers were evident. They seemed to be asleep to anything that lay outside of their comfort zone. Upset by the caustic remarks and continual undercurrent of cynicism I witnessed in the business world, I grew restless.

At the same time, I now had to deal with the stigma of having been in a mental hospital. I suppose my coworkers weren't sure what I'd do next. I'm sure stories had been circulated. God only knows what they'd heard or surmised. Was I going to be a marked individual forever? This began to weigh heavily on me and I worried that no one was going to want to be around me. To make matters worse, my heart was still broken from my split with David. Still, the cosmic door had cracked open and light continued to shine in, when I most needed it, in small yet miraculous ways.

One day at work, feeling despondent about David, I opened the morning mail to find a Land's End catalogue. On the cover were two stadium blankets. One was monogrammed with the name David. The other had the word "sunshine" embroidered on it. David had always called me Sunshine, the only person who ever did. When I saw those two personalized blankets, a sense of peace and love instantly permeated my entire being. It felt as if the universe had delivered a special message just for me. Another day at work, still trying to get my head back after all the meds I had been given during that first week in the hospital, I went into the ladies room to have some private time away from the office chatter. I felt so melancholy; so unlike the happy, positive self I had always been. For the very first time, I stood head to head with a part of me that was new and unknown. An indescribable sadness welled up inside of me. *What was it all about?* I wondered, as I thought of all the nights that I had cried myself to sleep. I'd never felt emotions as deep as those I was experiencing of late. *Could it be that Dr. Richards was right after all? Maybe I really was bi-polar or schizophrenic.*

I decided to see if I could really connect with this intense feeling of malaise and delve deeper into it to see what might happen. After all, what did I have to lose? I'd already experienced what could happen if I lost my mind. I must have been a sorry sight, sitting on that little stool in the ladies room, my head in my hands, as I gave into the pain and allowed it to sear right through me.

Dear God, I whispered, *Please help me. I feel so bad and my heart is so broken. Please let me know that this is not all there is to life—this terrible heartache and a 9 to 5 job that's boring as hell.*

And then something totally unexpected happened. Within seconds, I felt a divine radiance light up my entire body, as my awareness expanded. Instantly, my sadness was swept away as this astonishing feeling flooded through me, leaving me whole and complete again. I know it sounds impossible; if it hadn't happened to me I might not believe it either. But in no more time than it takes a light bulb to flash, it felt as if an unseen hand had fused the broken pieces of my heart back together. It was as if I had been touched by the hand of God and instantly returned to a state of physical, mental and emotional wholeness, right there in the corporate washroom.

Increasingly over the years, such glimpses and even sustained periods of heightened awareness have occurred both spontaneously and at will. What I realize now is that it's all around us; we just have to integrate and balance it. I believe that we are currently living in this heightened reality. The new energies that are becoming a part of our planetary existence are more refined, more elevated in their consciousness. To successfully navigate the uncertain aspects of our daily lives, I've found it essential to learn how to integrate one's intuitive abilities and spiritual understandings with everyday activities, like going to work, paying bills, socializing with friends and even going to the gym or yoga class. But within me was a growing urge to question, explore and develop an inner life, a life of connection to something larger. I had always believed in God but was beginning to question who or what that God meant to me. There were subtle signs, almost mysterious occurrences that led me to believe in something beyond my five senses. Daily miracles—ones that you might easily miss if you were in too much of a hurry or dismiss as coincidence—would occur during the course of my day: a line in a book I happened upon that answered an internal query, an old friend calling to offer support out of the blue, an inner knowing that some choice I was making was right. I began to have internal hunches that proved to be correct, and feelings about people's intentions that later were spot-on to the realities that presented themselves. So, the greatest gift from this time in my life—with Hemingway and Mr. Higgins as my spiritual tour guides—was not simply a belief in God, which I'd always had, but an experienced reality of what God really is. From then on, I had an unwavering connection to the God inside me, and to something much greater than myself: the world around me, all of life, and the cosmos.

Watch for synchronicities/miracles.

4.

Princess Di's Dance Class

It's a good thing my car was stolen.

Sure, I was upset at first. Then I thought of a way to turn the situation into a positive. On a whim, I used the reimbursement check from my theft insurance to buy an airline ticket to London where my older sister, Michele, and her family were living at the time. Growing up, Michele and I seemed to move in different worlds. We fought as siblings often do, but I always looked up to her; she was smart, popular, beautiful and her teachers loved her. Although I followed in her footsteps during my years of schooling, it was soon after that we veered in our own directions. After my hospital stay and the years that followed, my interests diverged from my siblings. I spent the greater share of my personal time exploring metaphysical precepts. Michele and her husband tried their best to understand what had happened to me, yet they never really understood my experience. So, taking a respite in London gave me a chance to talk more openly with them about this, and it was also a perfect opportunity to get out from under the watchful eyes of those who knew about my "mood awakening episode" and begin afresh.

So off I went to England to spend a few months with Michele, her handsome, accomplished husband, Chris, their newborn son, Spencer, and three-year-old daughter, Anne. It was a wonderful choice for me at the time. London has always held a bit of allure for me, with its lush parks, ancient streets and quaint architecture. The vast and noble British history permeates the very air. I knew I would only be staying for a few months, and I planned to take full advantage of the grand opportunity that awaited me—with side trips for adventure and leisurely jogs in Hyde Park to clear my head and strengthen my heart.

So, Michele, her kids and I would lunch in the neighborhood parks on peanut butter, banana and sprout sandwiches, and ride the lift with the nanny. Some days, I had the distinct pleasure of escorting Anne (who I affectionately call MFH, or My Favorite Human), to her weekly dance class. Just around the block in Knightsbridge, past the flower shop and up the stone steps, we would arrive at the very same dance school that Princess Diana attended in her youth. The ballet mistress, well in her 70s, was very proper and regal. Her students were the off-spring of England's upper-crust. They were oh, so sweet, in pink tights and slippers. After Madame put her little protégés through the rigors of *plies, battements* and *tendus*, she would distribute sweeties, or miniature candies, to those children who listened most attentively and had the best manners.

London Calling

As I watched MFH twirl and curtsey with the other pint-size ballerinas, a primordial gladness rose up in me, as if the internal mechanisms of a combination lock were slowly being fit in place for a grand opening into my true vocation. That's when I had the first inkling of wanting to support children in new and empowering ways. I returned to the US several months later with a loosely sketched out idea of how classes in good nutrition and self-esteem, laced with manners and movement, could be spun into a neighborhood gathering place for children.

Back home, the search for meaning behind my episode continued. I sought ways to delve inwards—certain that within me was a bright path to explore. I learned about Transcendental Meditation through a male friend. Bob and I were introduced by Dana at a neighborhood tavern that she and I would occasionally visit after work.

"Wow! You're glowing!" he said in greeting. "What's your body temperature?"

Was it a cheesy pick-up line? No, he saw inside me.

I was still aglow from my wake-up call. Purposely off alcohol to heighten my sensitivities and awareness, I was drinking vodka and OJ without the vodka.

"Really, take your temperature when you go home. I bet you're running high. Your eyes and face have light. Do you buzz? Do you meditate?" His questions flowed rapid fire, his eyes danced.

Bob was the gift I had been praying for: a person who lived beyond his five senses who could help me understand what had happened to me. We became unlikely lovers. Bob was a fair-haired, burly construction worker who liked motorcycles, leather jackets and camping. I'd never been with anyone like him before or since. One time, we took a camping trip to Virginia with other cycling enthusiasts. I am not a camper, nor do I enjoy roughing it. And six hours riding on the back of a Ducatti was certainly something new for me. I kept falling asleep on the back of Bob's motorcycle, sliding to the side until the awkward angle woke me up while going 60 mph on the freeway south.

But Bob was just what I needed at the time. Through him, I formally learned to meditate, got involved in TM and discovered other mind-body techniques. I was in my element with him. Increasingly, as I opened more and more to TM, I saw my episode as something to be embraced and nurtured, rather than something to be ashamed of. I wondered how many other people were in the same boat. *How many of them might be young children?* What I needed to do, I learned, was to integrate and balance my psychic abilities within my everyday existence, and be selective about whom I discussed them with, because clearly not everyone was open to it. The thought crossed my mind: *If only children could be taught this from the very beginning.* In time, of course, I discovered that this way of being wasn't new at all; it was simply that most of us have forgotten or learned to cover up our simple God-given abilities. Then I began to wonder: *if all babies are born with this, why do we forget?* The answer was clear: *we forget or learn to cover up in order to fit in and feel accepted.* Looking back on my life, how many times had I turned my back on this natural ability in order to fit in or to make others feel comfortable? In retrospect, perhaps, I did have a deeper knowing that that school morning in 11th grade was the last time I would lay eyes on my father. Hadn't I always been able to read and understand deeper meanings into why people acted in certain ways? Wasn't I able to make real many of my dreams as a child? I spent a lot of my childhood in fantasy-filled reveries, with imaginary friends and stuffed animals whose feelings and conversation kept me joyful company. I seemed to have a deeper understanding of my parents' actions and that they were doing their best with what understandings they had. I even enjoyed regular intuitions of what was to come. Like the time I wished for a new bike. One that was special, unusual. Within a few days of making this wish, my favorite

Scottish "uncle" Rab had arrived at our house with a grape-purple, antique three-wheeler just for me, for no apparent reason. It wasn't my birthday. Christmas had long gone. It was a ride like none other.

Steadily, as I practiced TM, I learned to assimilate my expanded state of consciousness into everyday living. I was anxious to research and develop the inner "calling" I had felt in London at MFH's dance class. I read countless books on topics ranging from psycho-cybernetics, body awareness, organic eating and yoga to alternative family celebrations and children's emotional and physical education. Writings on alternative topics weren't quite as prevalent back then as they are nowadays but I scoured whatever I could get my hands on: *The Richest Man in Babylon, Be Here Now, As a Man Thinketh, Bhagavad Gita* and another childhood favorite, *A Wrinkle in Time.* Whenever I could, I attended seminars to learn from others who were in the know. I took everything I had experienced and learned—my personal development interests, the tools and techniques that I acquired about breathing, meditation and visualization, and the power of the mind to create our realities—and started fashioning them into classes, workshops and "learning circles" for children of all ages. After what I'd just been through, coupled with the loss of my father at an early age, gratitude continued to fill me—a feeling of not wanting to take anything for granted, and for not taking things personally. My personal watchwords were humility, faith, trust and, above all, kindheartedness. And because I had a constant pipeline to my inner child and whimsical nature, it became easy to name my burgeoning venture Kids at Heart.

I spent months reading, meditating, researching, visualizing, writing class curriculum, securing a commercial building to rent, designing the flow of the physical space and room décor that supported the act of self-discovery for children, initiating advertising ideas and networking with others who offered classes and activities for children. I sought out and aligned with child development specialists, counselors, physicians and doctors at hospitals and universities, and put together a board of advisors that brought to the table all the areas of child-oriented expertise that I didn't have. Looking back I am amazed at how easily it all seemed to come together. Perhaps it was the strength of my belief in what I was doing that opened doors so easily. Or perhaps it was simply my naivety (or chutzpah?). Either way, I simply targeted the professionals I wanted to have on my board, called them up, met with them and enlisted their help. Astonishingly, everyone I contacted—from psychiatrists to PhDs in child development—was willing and able to come on board. In the process I discovered that I had a knack for enlisting people's support and I felt energized by collaborating with others.

As I went on, serendipity tended to occur more often and with tangible positive consequences. Around this time, I started putting intention-setting into practice. My last order of business before opening to the public was finding a financially savvy individual whose skills

Never underestimate the power of declaring your intent.

would complement mine. I wanted to find someone who was good with numbers, preferably a young woman my age with a spiritual persuasion. I intended for this person to be adventurous, willing to take a chance on something new and unseen and, above all, someone who was not afraid to be silly and off-beat when the "job" called for it. Together, we would have everything required to develop and operate a small business with a never-done-before concept for kids.

As if custom delivered by the universe, my future-perfect business ally and now dearest friend, Jennifer, soon turned up—and in the most unusual circumstances.

Two Kids at Heart
By then, I was an active TM student and decided to sign up for an advanced course in Washington, DC. Everything was set for the Kids at Heart opening eight weeks later… except I hadn't yet met my desired business manager. Jennifer had flown down from Boston for the same course. Our paths were about to cross in a way that symbolizes the joy and levity that our friendship continues to be blessed with to this day.

So there we were at the TM course, down in a basement filled with bed cushions where we went twice each day to learn a flying mantra. The idea is to meditate on this mantra and eventually "fly" as birds do. This may sound unusual but the ancient seers and gurus who practice yogic principles have actually trained their bodies to be so in sync with their focused, calm minds that they are able to accomplish acts that are beyond our human reasoning. One of these abilities is to raise one's body off the ground while cross-legged in a meditative trance through a sort of hopping action, which TM devotees call flying. As you can imagine, it takes a lot of practice. You can be at the course for an entire week and maybe, just maybe, you get the hang of it by the time you leave. When it does happen, most people giggle or laugh out loud. It's a silly but joyful feeling. Once you get going, you pull out of your little spot and go around the room, hopping (while in a lotus position) from cushion to cushion.

All of a sudden, I hopped right in front of Jennifer. Without missing a beat, we immediately started bouncing, boom, boom, boom, around the room together. Right from the start, Jennifer and I were in sync.

I later learned that Jennifer lived in Boston, where she worked for an international accounting firm. When she admitted that she was unsure what she wanted to do long term, I told her about my idea for a health club for kids in Pittsburgh. Jennifer was intrigued.

"Maybe I could learn how to operate a Kids at Heart center and eventually open a franchise in my hometown of Cape Cod," she ventured.

And that was it. Jennifer immediately returned home, packed everything she could fit into her little blue Chevette and sold the rest with the thought that, at least if she had her car, she could get back to the Cape should it not work out.

Jennifer moved to Pittsburgh and has never left.

Six weeks after she arrived there, we opened the doors of Kids at Heart with big ideas, a clever phone number (884-KIDS) and 100 children. I am forever grateful that Jennifer decided to throw all caution to the wind to help me start my business. As the months and years progressed, we became best friends. To this day, she remains my closest friend, business mentor, inspiration and loving support arm.

Within a year, with one location open, I was ready to take my show on the road and seek funding to expand my venture. I contacted the Pittsburgh Public Schools, numerous private schools in the area, libraries, museums and many other philanthropic entities. We began scheduling school assembly programs, all designed to get the word out to families about the offerings at Kids at Heart. I also set up meetings with Pittsburgh-based corporations and universities such as Blue Cross/Blue Shield and Carnegie-Mellon University. For a meeting with General Nutrition Center, I had my graphic artist sketch a mock Kids at Heart kiosk, complete with kid-tested and parent-approved vitamins, supplements and coloring/recipe books.

🦋 *Don't let doubts undermine your dreams or determination.*

They loved it because children's vitamins and supplements were virtually nonexistent at that time. I also met with the television staff from ABC children's programming, as well as Pittsburgh's Family Communications.

Do I make this all sound easy? How was I able to get in front of important people in world renowned organizations so quickly? Quite simply, because I didn't know that I couldn't. I just didn't consider the unlikely nature of not being able to fulfill my intentions. My focus was on the result, so I did whatever it took to accomplish it. I believe that my combined confidence and innocence was due in part to my mystical episode. After that period of heightened awareness, life in the "regular" world seemed even less intimidating. So I happily plodded forward in my own little world of all possibilities.

As I went about networking and explaining the Kids at Heart concept, some people gave me the most perplexed look. "Why on earth would you combine nutrition classes with self-esteem exercises?" they'd ask. Remember, this was before Gymboree, Chuck E. Cheese's Pizza Time Theatre, My Gym, Discovery Zone and many of the other play and enrichment centers for children. It was also a shade before the "we are what we eat" era of nutrition counseling and the mainstreaming of organics. There was, of course, Emily Post's venerable etiquette classes for children; however, no one at the time was teaching compassionate ways of being, visualization/affirmations, positive thinking, child empowerment and kind-heartedness combined with fitness, NEWtrition, manners and self-esteem activities in an enjoyable, modern-day environment. Kids at Heart rolled it all together under one roof.

My mom understood more than anyone what it meant for me to do my own thing, to prove I wasn't "mad" after all. In the ensuing months, she became my biggest fan and most ardent supporter. She offered words of support, ideas for mascot names, marketing angles and a hug or glance filled with admiration when I needed it most. Because Jennifer was focused on the financials, setting up our corporate infrastructure and still holding on to her part-time job, I trained a staff of six by myself. We had cute apron uniforms made, and commissioned a local artist to decorate and paint a healthy snack vending contraption called the Scrumption Machine. His original, empowering artwork adorned the walls and cardboard stand up mascot characters enhanced the space, all with the goal to promote healthy, loving ways of being in the world.

I also developed walk-around character mascots for our school assembly programs and to lead the exercise classes. Sweet Harmony the Hippo had matching pink legwarmers and sweatband *a la* Jane Fonda, who was hot at the time. Sweet Harmony was big and fat, yet loved herself just as she was, always striving to be the best she could be with what she had. There was such a media push at the time to be thin, with stick figure models and TV personalities. I wanted children to understand that they are perfect and whole just they way they are. "I like you just as you are" were the endearing words of my homegrown Pittsburgh hero, Fred Rogers of *Mister Roger's Neighborhood.* And there was Good Stuff the Bear, who prepared healthy snacks and wore a chef's hat adorned with a big heart. He knew the importance of cooking and handling food with love. Mom came up with the name Properly Tot for a sweet, little frog who taught good manners. The Sweet Hearts were little pink heart figures with dangly legs and arms who, in the pages of our coloring book, gave free hugs with squeals of delight.

Since my guiding principles were peace, love, harmony and joy, infused with spiritual tenets from various universal religions and futurist philosophies about our potential as human beings, it was only natural that I incorporate those aspects into my business for children. Parts of my daily spiritual practice—mainly meditation and the use of visualization and affirmations—not only kept me focused, aligned and happily on my path, it also became apparent that our youth might benefit from them. I would put on audio headphones and listen for hours to my own voice and music tapes that I made. These

🦋 Audio tapes, affirmations and visualizations are powerful ways to program your unconscious mind toward success.

homemade tapes featured me stating in the present tense, as if it had already happened, the success of Kids at Heart, the multitude of children and parents who would attend, their positive experiences, financial backers and supporters who would join us, and the media attention that would naturally arise. I would further visualize the positive effects on the community and families as a result of Kids at Heart, and its small part in creating a kinder, gentler future generation. I thought, *What would my life have been like had I known these things as a child?* It became evident that this was a niche market in society just waiting to be actualized.

So often, we're told, "Oh, you can't do that" or "that will never happen" but Jennifer's and my attitude was "we can do anything!"

And, miraculously, we did.

Looking back, I don't believe that Jennifer and I would have had such a "can do" attitude if we hadn't had our own personal awakenings—she with her newfound courage to pick up and move sight unseen to another part of the country with nothing more than the contents of her little car, and me with my post-awakening integration process. Our daring to think big with Kids at Heart is what came out of our internal work.

We observed in awe as one by one our intentions started coming to fruition.

Out of the blue, we decided one day to call the *Tonight Show* in Los Angeles. We told them we were coming out and asked if they might

> 🦋 *Become aware of self-limiting beliefs and start changing your thinking. Believing in the possible creates space for potential.*

want to have us on the show while we were out there. Then we called *Hour Magazine* with Gary Collins, which was a popular show at the time, and told them we were flying out to be on the *Tonight Show.* We had no money and no connections but we wanted to get to Hollywood because we had this idea of a Kids at Heart television show and wanted to meet with agents and learn about franchising.

We got a return call from *Hour Magazine* saying they wanted us first. So, they paid for me to fly out and put me up in a hotel. I appeared on the show. Poor Jen had to fly out on a red eye because they would only pay for the one ticket. We were so naive that we didn't know we could have a second person in my paid-for hotel room, so every time room service came by Jen would hide under the bed. We spent the rest of our stay drinking champagne by the pool and basking in the California sun. It was like a dream, a fantasy come true. And it was a revelation to know that it's not only possible to live like that... but that it could happen to us!

In fact, it felt as if we were being guided throughout our entire trip. For example, our neighborhood policeman, who helped with our leasehold improvements in his off-time, also had a brother who was a Hollywood agent. He made a call and we were given an opportunity to meet with his younger brother. So there we were, dressed in suits and heels, walking up this steep hill on our way to the meeting. We were sweating and our feet hurt. Then a man walked by in a business suit and said, "You're almost there!" We thought, wow, we ARE almost there.

As Jen and I have often discussed since, when you start to live with an attitude of fun, of flow, of "anything's possible," of knowing that guidance is always available, the support you need suddenly starts to come from everywhere. As Jen says: "It's such a way to live! Why would we want to live any other way?" And when you have like-minded friends who mirror it back to you, it becomes even stronger. When you stop saying: "I can't do that," and start saying: "I wonder *how* I could

✎ Change your thinking, change the outcome.

do that," everything changes. You go from a place of shutting off possibility to creating the space for potential. And when you choose to live in a place of potential anything can happen. Once you flip your attitude in this way, it becomes a question of "how good are you willing to have it?" It's a choice. Once you make that choice, what you want comes to you automatically.

Yes, we can choose to live in the "other" reality, the one in which people believe "it can't be done." People make the choice to live in that reality all the time. They say things like, "Oh, it's such a gloomy day," or "Oh, I had a terrible thing happen to me today," and they take those choices into themselves. It becomes their life. Then one day, perhaps they choose differently. And life becomes something more. For those of us who do decide to choose differently, life becomes more inviting, exciting, and potentially richer with experience.

That's exactly what happened to me. On the heels of my mood awakening, I had suddenly decided to follow my intuition and choose differently. There were those who did not approve of my taking a leave of absence from work, cashing in my insurance money and taking off for England for several months. But gifting myself with distance and time away from those speculative glances is what brought me the first of many golden opportunities to combine my talents and desire to do good in the world alongside a caring, loving colleague. It had all been supremely arranged to bring me exactly what I had needed at that time: a new lease on life and a new view of living that was much larger than anything I had imagined before that summer of '81.

So my car being stolen really was grand theft auto, with the emphasis on the word *grand*.

5.

Fingertips in the Trash Can

It's not a sight you see every day in the boardrooms of corporate America. Sweet Harmony the Hippo in her pink fitness gear ensconced between two of the world's most highly respected billionaire philanthropists and business leaders.

And it's not an experience I encountered every day, either, being welcomed into the stately executive suite of The Hillman Company, a real estate, venture capital and medical technology conglomerate based in Pittsburgh. Months earlier, I had contacted the offices of philanthropist and Republican Party activist Elsie Hillman—cousin of Barbara Bush and close advisor to the Bush family—after a brief introduction through a friend of a friend who'd worked with Elsie on George Bush, Sr.'s political campaign. In my gut, I felt that Elsie would really get the Kids at Heart concept and want to support it—a far out possibility, to be sure, but by this time I was becoming increasingly comfortable in the anything-can-happen realm. So much so, that I had taken it completely in my stride when, lickety-split, Elsie's assistant got back to me with a date for a meeting. Once again, my instincts had proved correct. Now Elsie had called me in for a second pitch meeting with another key person she wanted me to meet.

From a distance, I had admired Elsie. She appeared to be family oriented, with a twinkle in her eye and social concerns in her heart. She and her billionaire husband, Henry L. Hillman—both beloved faces on the landscape of Pittsburgh and beyond—would often be seen out and about doing their own grocery shopping and such. I once saw them picking up a large turkey and all the trimmings one afternoon before Thanksgiving at a market in the tony Pittsburgh neighborhood of Shadyside. She seemed down to earth, and I found this to be true in the various meetings and conversations I had with her. Henry (heir to a steel-and-coke fortune and ranked as one of the world's richest people by *Forbes)* had steered his family's firm for decades before stepping down as chairman in 2004. He and Elsie had raised four children. Through The Hillman Foundation, they have donated tens of millions of dollars over the years to cancer research and, in Pittsburgh alone, tens of millions more to Children's Hospital of Pittsburgh. Their largesse has also resulted in the building of the state-of-the-art Hillman Cancer Center at UPMC Shadyside Hospital in Pittsburgh, as well as the Hillman Library at the University of Pittsburgh, among other major contributions. Elsie is also a political *tour de force* who helped elect every Pennsylvania GOP office holder in the past 30 years—not to mention an American president. Nowadays, Elsie seems to focus more of her time on women's issues, the arts and the Pittsburgh region, but every statewide GOP candidate still turns to her for support.

"Henry! Look what I'm going to do for kids today!" Elsie announced at one point during the meeting when her husband poked his head around the door.

He glanced in my direction. I sat up tall, hands crossed primly over my knees, smiling from ear to ear. At my side was a vivid cardboard mock-up of the Kids at Heart Scrumption Machine—filled with healthy snacks called Yibbly-Bits, Lisciousnips and Tummy Yums. On the boardroom table was a Kids at Heart kiosk mock up, along with sample snack packages and fanciful, life-size cutouts of our mascots. The colorful designs and childlike figures made for a wonderfully puzzling display for Henry to see, unlike what he typically saw in his boardroom, I'm sure.

"Um… how nice!" Henry said in a somewhat bemused fashion.

Elsie had called the meeting because she believed that Kids at Heart could be the perfect children's addition to Weight Watchers, one of the strongest international brands of Pittsburgh-based H. J. Heinz Company, a leading global food processor with operations in 200-plus countries. Hence, the presence of her very good friend and colleague Dr. Anthony O'Reilly at our second meeting. Impressively, at age 37, Tony had become president and chief operating officer of Heinz worldwide, and by the time I met him in 1983, he was the CEO of H. J. Heinz Company. (Four years later, he was elected the first-ever, non-family-member chairman, succeeding H. J. Heinz II, grandson of the founder. Under his leadership, Heinz subsequently metamorphosed into a major international competitor and its value increased 15-fold.)

In preparation for the meeting, I had read up on this Dublin-born billionaire of many talents. As a young lad, Tony rose to fame in Ireland and Great Britain as a record-scoring rugby player for several national teams. Among other ventures as a young businessman, he had bought into Independent News and Media and, as its eventual chairman, pushed the company to increase its reach in Ireland and expand into other national markets. Married to Greek shipping heiress and thoroughbred horse breeder Chryss Goulandris, he has six children. His O'Reilly Foundation has donated substantial monies to fund libraries in Dublin and provide scholarships to Irish university students. He also served as a director of The New York Stock Exchange.

So there I was, a wide-eyed, twenty-something wannabe entrepreneur sitting across from the benevolent Elsie Hillman and this dashing silver-haired Irishman—surrounded by big, foam-core figures of Sweet Harmony, Good Stuff and Properly Tot. Earlier, I had made the difficult decision to keep the Sweet Heart dolls at home. It pained me to leave them out of the fun but it was the smart thing to do. I probably wouldn't have been able to hold it together if the esteemed Sir O'Reilly (yes, he was knighted in 2001 by Queen Elizabeth II) picked up one of those dangly legged, pink-heart figures and started to play with it.

Thankfully, I was far too excited to be nervous. From the moment I walked in the room my presentation flowed splendidly. Elsie had obviously familiarized herself with the Kids at Heart story and knew my promotional materials like the back of her palm. At one point I leaned back and listened in awe as she explained the concept to Tony. She gushed. He listened. We discussed. She then gushed some more. He nodded. Then he buzzed his secretary and asked her to place a call to the president of Weight Watchers in New York. Within minutes he was on the other line. Tony told him to expect my call to discuss a Kids at Heart collaboration.

Tony and Elsie were both so kind, so generous with their time—and so wealthy, yet seemed to handle their positions with compassion and groundedness. I was moved by that. And I was thankful for the coveted position I was in. Many people requested (and still request) meetings with these individuals and never get the opportunity; and there I sat, showcasing my dream. It was the high point of my young professional life, one that I will always remember with fondness.

"If I die tomorrow, I'll go with a huge smile on my face," I later said to Jennifer about the meeting.

The outcome of that meeting was a follow-up appointment with the then president of Weight Watchers. Chuck Berger. I was flown to New York City with my mascot cutouts, Scrumption snacks and best professional personage in tow. That meeting could not have been more different than the one I'd had with Tony and Elsie. From the moment I launched into my pitch, it was clear that Chuck was only meeting with me as a favor to the higher ups. He was totally uninterested. He was checked out, somewhere else, not even listening. Have you ever been in a situation with someone and you know they're not present? His attitude oozed a dismissive what-you-have-to-say-is-of-no-consequence-to-me-whatsoever air, as if to say: "*Who do you think you are* to even be in my office?"

It was so blatantly rude that I vowed that very day to NEVER do that to another person in my work or personal life—to always give others my undivided attention. I walked out of that New York skyscraper head down, shoulders slumped, Sweet Harmony tucked under my arm—and wanting to submerge myself in river water like real hippos do. I knew when I left Chuck Berger's office that nothing more would come of it. I followed up by sending a bouquet of flowers to Tony with a thank-you note that said: "Kids at Heart is all abloom! Thanks for supporting my ideas for a WW for kids!" I never heard a response and the Weight Watchers idea withered on the vine. I was disheartened but not unfamiliar with rejection. Since then, I've come to view rejection as just another opportunity to be creative with my intention-setting.

But I didn't stay down for long. Within a month, good news arrived in the form of a phone call from Elsie. She'd set up another meeting with a representative from the Heinz family's personal estate. This time, she wouldn't be accompanying me to the meeting. She had already given them background on Kids at Heart and her seal of approval. I guess in her mind it was a done deal. I met with Dixon Brown, a respected representative and overseer of the Heinz family fortune. Elsie had asked them to match her contribution to fund Kids at Heart. And with little ado, they did. Dixon presented me with a check for $100,000 from Mr. Heinz, Sr.

I was amazed, shocked and so appreciative that the Hillmans and Mr. Heinz had offered $200,000 in funding for the Kids at Heart expansion. In my heart, I had known it would all come together some day, I just hadn't known how. So I had just kept on doing what I did best, selling my heart out on something I believed in. And I had been lucky enough to have my wishes fall on receptive ears and very big hearts.

Jennifer and I used the monies to build out our second company-owned location, hire staff, brand the concept, produce a marketing campaign and pay some salaries. It was all remarkable, a time of innocence, big dreams and the courage to just go for it—fueled by a higher connection that was escalating day by day.

All the while, Elsie continued to support my venture in ways that may seem small in retrospect but were hugely important to me. On occasion, she would take me to lunch. A handsome woman with dark, well-groomed features and conservative, tasteful style, Elsie was easy to be with, a good conversationalist. She was kind to the restaurant staff and quick to laugh at her forgetful nature. Of course, Elsie always insisted that she pay for lunch. In my still-young eyes, it amazed me that a billionaire would use a little change purse to house her pennies, nickels and dimes. I got a kick out of watching her dip into that little satchel and pull out small coins. I guess I assumed she dealt only in hundreds and fifties. Funny what you think.

Elsie connected me with The Hillman Company's senior vice president of business development, who was gracious, patient and spent many hours with me over the course of many weeks. I became more and more knowledgeable a budgets, business plans, action steps and protocol.

I was also given full access to The Hillman Company's executive offices to utilize their copy and production center. After weeks of fine tuning the freshly written Kids at Heart business plan for expansion, I was ready to print copies and bind it for circulation to potential corporate sponsors, investors or advisory potentials. So, there I was in Hillman's executive copy center with state-of-the-art printing equipment, and lots of it. I must have looked like a kid in a candy shop amidst the mega-technology. It was a veritable Kinko's in there. I was given a personal tour of their warehouse-size print shop by a friendly man named Hans, who, I later learned, was a respected long-time employee of the company. Hans was eager and proud to enlighten me about the inner workings of the print facility, his sole domain as senior manager of the print and copy shop. I could tell he'd given that tour hundreds of times. Towards the end, we arrived at the *piece de resistance*. Like a proud father introducing his first born child, Hans paused dramatically. Then, when he was sure he had my full attention, he waved his hand with a flourish in front of a gleaming new piece of machinery.

"Now THIS," whispered Hans "is my pride and joy. It was just delivered last week."

I looked at Hans, expectantly.

Hans looked at the machine reverently.

His eyes softened. "It's an electric paper cutter."

To understand what a big deal this was, you have to remember that this was back in the 80s, when electric paper cutters and shredders were rare. I was impressed they even had one.

Seeing that I was suitably impressed, Hans eagerly offered to show me how to use the paper cutter.

With his face turned towards me to make sure I was observing closely, Hans started his demonstration.

"You simply slide the edges here, press this button and…"

And…

Then the unthinkable happened.

My gaze of interest slowly froze into a mask of horror as the brand new, razor sharp cutting blade descended—not onto the sheaf of paper that should have been there, and wasn't, but right over Hans' fingertips.

Hans gasped.

I winced.

Hans frantically tried to hide what had happened. How could he? Blood was squirting everywhere. .

I put my hands over my mouth and inwardly screamed ARGHH! I was at a total loss to know what to do. Should I call for help? Get him some antiseptic? Or curl up and die as fast as possible? Hans didn't know what to do, either. His embarrassment must have taken precedence over whatever shock and pain he must have been feeling, because I couldn't believe what he did next.

He put his uninjured hand down on the counter and, as casually as if he was sweeping potato peelings into the garbage disposal, simply whisked those bloody tips right into the trash can. Off they went. Deep six-ed. Discarded like so many plastic spiral-binding coils.

I mentally panicked: *Oh my God, here I am already feeling somewhat out of place, just a young lass from down the block trying to start a small business that helps kids, who's been granted the miracle of entrée to this high-tech, billion dollar corporate headquarters, and now my name is going to be all over the company as someone who caused an esteemed manager to sever his fingertips!*

All I had wanted was to get in and get out of that copy center without causing any trouble to anyone during their already busy, deadline-filled days. Then this! A popular company man maims himself on my behalf! The last thing I wanted was to be labeled a trouble-maker. Ugh, blood was splattered everywhere. I wanted to become invisible, to slip out of the building unnoticed, and never come back.

Equally mortified, Hans quickly wrapped his bloody hand in a paper towel and excused himself. I quickly made my escape without saying anything to anyone. What would I say and to whom would I say it? Months later, when I heard that Hans was no longer with the company, I didn't know what to think. I felt oddly responsible for his departure. Hans, if you're out there, I hope you went on to brighter days, with or without your fingertips. (They grow back, don't they?)

Around this time I met my soon-to-be-husband, Larry—a seasoned, successful businessman who taught me much during the 18 years that followed about life, love, business and the ultimate pursuit of happiness. I remember when I first laid eyes on Larry. I was seated at a restaurant awaiting the rest of my dinner party with a friend. Larry turned the corner of the dimly lit lounge attired in a dashing silk sport coat and tie that flapped with every quick, fit step he took. I was immediately drawn to him (and he later told me I was "cute as a button"). His eyes danced like the charming Irishman he was. His gaze casually caught mine and I was at once taken with his air of charm and *joie de vivre*. Larry knew my friend and, surprised to see him, paused at our table and happily announced that he was there to celebrate his mother's 90th birthday. As our eyes finally locked, Larry smiled a big smile. My heart warmed as I thought to myself, *Now there's a happy, confident individual.* That, in a nutshell, was Larry's MO: happy and confident. Through those attributes, he was able to nurture a legion of adoring friends and colleagues, amass a fortune and always be up for a good time. He was also a very generous, well-meaning spirit. I so admired him and grew to love him deeply.

After that evening, I met Larry again on the eve of Valentine's Day at that same restaurant with a neighbor and a friend for a casual, non-date dinner. We all had a lovely time. Larry was gracious and jovial, including everyone in the conversation. He asked about my life with genuine interest and happily picked up the check for all of us. The next day, I sent a bouquet of flowers to his office with a card that simply read: "Encore." (He kept that card in his wallet during all of our years together, perhaps even beyond.) After our first official date, we went back to his apartment for a nightcap and after one kiss, I never left his side for the next 18 years.

Larry was excited about my work with Kids at Heart and in a show of love and support, decided to invest in the venture, also. By then, Kids at Heart was operating regular, ongoing classes in fitness, nutrition, manners and self-esteem in both locations for all ages through the teen years. We had received 87 requests for franchises from across the country as a result of media coverage and the appearance I had made on national television. We were well on our way to growing a solid business and spreading goodness, just as I had envisioned.

After two years working with Kids at Heart Jennifer made the decision to leave for broader horizons with her soon-to-be-husband and their dream of starting a company of their own. She had successfully accomplished for me what she does best in any work environment: she had supported my creative process and put a firm financial infrastructure in place for the company. From then on, I was doing everything: teaching classes, training facilitators, compiling accounting records, promoting the concept, devising marketing plans, garnering funding interest and researching franchise options. But I missed the camaraderie I had with Jennifer, her willingness to pitch in and help with everything, and her valuable financial understanding. In time, the second location began to put a drain on our profitability. While its location in a popular strip mall gave us desirable visibility, membership wasn't growing fast enough to meet monthly rental fees. Although the loyal moms of our pint-sized members willingly staged community fundraisers to support the higher rental rates, revenues still weren't enough to cover monthly expenses, support franchise growth and fund the necessary staffing positions that were vital to keeping everything on an even keel. Just like some of the youngsters we were nurturing inside the Kids at Heart centers, we had encountered our own growing pains. I needed to configure new marketing, funding and membership plans.

Then, personal tragedy struck once more.

"Mom's had a stroke," my brother Bill announced over the phone.

I was stunned. "How could this be? She's only in her early 60s." Mom was in very good health. In fact, the stroke had occurred while she was exercising at a local health spa. She had simply slumped to the floor and never regained consciousness.

For eleven intensely difficult days, I sat with Mom as she lay in a coma. My emotions were all over the place. I wrestled to resolve past issues within myself about our relationship as mother and daughter. You see, after my father's sudden passing, I had become my mom's constant companion, her only local female daughter and her social director. While I enjoyed going places with her in the evenings, brainstorming ideas for Kids at Heart together, and going with her to her exercise center, over time, things began to get a little awkward. Mom became increasingly dependent on me. She started to drink more than she was accustomed to. And with little other than me in the way of companionship, life became lonely and somewhat boring for her. Once I met Larry and my attention was more divided, she found it harder to cope well on her own. That, coupled with the fact that Larry was the same age as her (which she had found very difficult to accept), had gradually created a small rift between us. We eventually weathered that storm as she grew to accept Larry but, as often happens at times like this, all the buried guilt and self-recriminations began to surface. Given Mom's state of unconsciousness, I had no opportunity to tell her how sorry I was for anything I might have said or done that may have hurt her in any way.

So instead, I decided to use my intuitive strengths to commune lovingly with her spirit. I read her poems. I cried. I talked to her. The lines of our one-sided conversations blurred. I was speaking to myself. I was speaking to her spirit. I was speaking to no one at all. And I was speaking to All That Is. I prayed for confirmation that I was reaching Mom on some level. I got it. One day, the on-call nurse told me that Mom's vital signs consistently improved after I'd spent hours with her. In the end, though, it wasn't enough.

On the twelfth day, my brothers, sister and I jointly agreed to take Mom off life support. With that decision, I assumed the worst was over. I was wrong.

I went into a tailspin. My mother's death at such a young and vibrant age seemed to call up my father's, along with all the grief that I'd managed to stuff deep down. And besides, I was exhausted from putting so much of my time and energies into building Kids at Heart. I retreated into a quiet sadness, and all I wanted to do was spend time alone or with Larry. I needed time to retreat and deal with it. I just needed time. Suddenly, the continual pressures of a growing a business seemed overwhelming. From the nadir of deep sorrow, I made a gut-wrenching decision. I closed both Kids at Heart centers and put the business on hold until I regained my balance.

I spent the next year or so focused more on family matters than business. Larry and I had begun living together and I wanted to focus on our relationship. He was wonderfully supportive of me during that time, but I couldn't take Kids at Heart entirely off life support, too. I did what could be done with it. The programs we had offered were solid and well-received, so I took our tried-and-true curriculum and developed it into curriculum kits for school assemblies and for retail sale at local bookstores. The idea of a Kids at Heart television show was always in the back of my mind, so I explored that option. I started by making contact with one of Larry's colleagues who worked in TV production. Larry had become a silent partner in a local ad agency, and this gentleman—Russ Streiner—had been contracted to do some video production for the agency. With help from Russ, who worked on the famed *Night of the Living Dead* movie with George Romero, I produced a TV pilot that eventually aired on Pittsburgh ABC affiliate WTAE-TV. Because the show was well received, the network wanted to continue partnering with us, and Shop 'N Save, the local grocery chain, had signed on as sponsors; however, the TV station wanted creative control. I said no and immediately took off to New York and California to meet with rival CBS. I called on everyone I knew who had anything to do with TV or children's programming, and through six degrees of separation, I usually would land a meeting or two with an executive. Sometimes, I got these meetings by just setting an intention and making phone call after phone call.

Then my nemesis appeared on the scene. He was huge. He was purple. He was a dinosaur… He was a massive phenomenon. His name was BARNEY.

And I couldn't bring myself to watch him on TV; it wasn't just the cheesy-corn. It reminded me of what could have been.

And still could, perhaps.

I closed the door on Kids at Heart for good. But the concept of empowering and educating America's youth in a mind-body-spirit way never really went away. It just lay quietly behind another door. Twenty years in the future, I would gain entry.

6.

The Cause of Me

With both my parents gone and my business venture a supposed flop (which is how I looked upon it at the time), I plunged into a period of intense self-doubt. It shook my faith base—faith in myself, faith in my ideals and, yes, even my faith in God. It's said that all spiritual seekers arrive at such a place. Why? Because living with expanded consciousness kicks away the status quo. Challenges come up every step of the way to test our faith. Thus it is continually necessary to question, to reflect, to ask… WHY? We tend to think of life's grading system as pass or fail. Good or bad. All or nothing. I've come to believe the opposite. The way I see it, we are continuously grading ourselves, *and* we are continually "passing" in various degrees. We are both teacher and student at the same time. And "fail" is not the four-letter-word we might think it is.

Periods of questioning can make us feel like the ground has shifted under our very feet, leaving us exposed to deeper, darker realities about the way things are. I had been a consistent meditator for at least five years; I had completed a number of self-improvement seminars, during which I had visualized, cleared, cleansed, purged, yoga-ed, re-birthed, surged and more. And yet, I felt tremulous. I had really believed that thoughts are powerful and our intentions are heard. This situation marked the first instance where *my* timeframe and *my* perspective on what accomplishment should look like for the completion and manifestation of my desires, and the universe's timeframe for its fruition, seemed to be on a different time track. *I do my very best,* I thought. *I turn my life over to God. I meditate. I set intentions and visualize. And I take real-world action to realize my goals. What more can I possibly do?*

Reflecting on this question during that period of time, I came to understand that there's a delicate balance between our ability to receive miracles when they come our way, and more importantly, to embrace what's in our life currently—whether we want it or not, because we don't always take the time to imagine the larger picture. If we were able to view our reality from an enlightened, expansive perspective, oftentimes we'd see that where we are is exactly where we need to be, or perhaps it's exactly what we've created for ourselves through our thoughts and feelings. "If you want to know the past, to know what has caused you, look at yourself in the present, for that is the past's effect," it says in the *Majjhima Nikaya* sutras. "If you want to know your future, then look at yourself in the present, for that is the cause of the future."

In other words, this is when I became very clear that all we have is the present moment. I was prepared to look at myself to define what "caused me" in the past and how my way of being in the present was creating my future. I knew it involved thankfulness for each experience, accepting and not fearing what happens to us, and living with a compassionate heart. I looked around and assessed what I was grateful for. Larry was at the top of the list.

I've heard it said that little girls grow up to marry a man like their father and Larry certainly reflected many of my Dad's qualities. He was a wonderful husband and generous man who freely shared his heart, mind, resources and *joie de vivre* with me and many others. I fell in love with his intellect, his wit and open mindedness. He was truly a renaissance man of the highest order who lived life to the fullest and shared his good fortune with others at every turn. He trusted life, people and the process of time, and treated everyone, regardless of status or station, with the same kind manner. And he made me feel safe. Larry loved me. He wanted to take care of me. And I was in a space where I needed to be taken care of. We made the decision to marry and I embraced my newfound role as wife, homemaker and instant step-mom.

The adage about marrying one's father doesn't say anything, though, about them being close in age! Larry was 32 years my senior. I sometimes wondered what my dad would have thought about his baby girl marrying a man the same age as her mother. Yikes. As I mentioned, it took my mom a while to come to terms with our relationship, which she finally had by the time she passed. It left Larry and me with a good feeling that we had her blessing. She knew that I was happy and that Larry was a good man. As a widow who never remarried, Mom would often quip in response to our dinner invitations: "Judy, if the three of us go out together, who are people going to think is with whom?" I think she was only half joking.

Larry's seven children, who ranged in age from their early 30s to two years older than me, were at first bemused by our age difference; however, they soon came to view me as simply Judy rather than step-mom. To the grandchildren, I was Grand-Judy. When we married, there were a dozen. Today, there are 25. In a blink, I had a clutch of young ones to dote on. I took to my new status like a duck to water. I ditched the business suit, donned an apron and hostess tiara, and found new purpose in crafting homemade cards and presents. Larry's family was respectful, good natured and appreciative, and I was happy to pour my creative energies into something so rewarding. The grandchildren came to visit often. We'd invite them for sleepovers and make popcorn and crafts. It always thrilled me to watch them in action and hang out with them. It filled me up with a kid vibe. How I loved that.

At our home, I had a fuzzy bear propped on our bed (that I bought for me! To this day, I love stuffed animals). One of the grandkids noticed that Mookie the bear didn't have eyes, and she asked me why. I remembered my favorite quote from *The Little Prince* and explained that he didn't need eyes because he saw from his heart.

At times, Larry's children misunderstood his business and social focus. When they were growing up, they said their father was rarely around. I empathized with them, as I knew well the feelings surrounding an absentee father. When they grew older, Larry would schedule visits with them within the structure of a party or other social event, so there was little one-on-one time. He may not have been able to see what he was doing through his children's eyes, but he loved and admired each of them, as well as his grandchildren, with all his heart.

During our 18 years together, Larry and I would often talk about his entrepreneurial endeavors. He was the epitome of a self-made man, building a business in the steel refractory field from the age of 24 into a multi-million-dollar enterprise. He then went on to purchase and invest in other businesses that spanned the hair care industry, advertising, waste management, pizza, tea, cows and fast food. All the while, he believed in the integrity of a gentlemanly handshake. Some called him gullible. I saw him as pure of heart and mind. Over the years, I watched as he artfully navigated the often choppy waters of deceit and political waywardness in his career. I saw them come and go: snappy dressers, fast talkers, quick-buck artists and seasoned egoists who tried to take advantage of Larry's good nature and deepening pockets. Regardless of the situation, he never spoke ill of anyone. He took his punches and got up swinging. We both believed that karma has a way of catching up with people; what goes around comes around eventually, even if we don't witness it ourselves. Larry was always light on his feet—both on the dance floor and in the boardroom.

I greatly admired Larry's business acumen and was inspired by it. With his loving encouragement, I continued to nurture my entrepreneurial spirit in various ways during our married years. It started with my love of golf—yes, like father, like daughter. Larry and I spent a lot of time on the links with family, friends and business associates. I enjoyed playing 18 holes in those beautiful, natural environments, the camaraderie and close friendships that evolved, and the skill and tenacity required in a game that, for me, closely mirrored the spiritual tenets of presence, patience, balance and humility. All this, and yet I absolutely couldn't stand wearing the women's golf attire on the market at that time. The styles were conservative, pedestrian, white bread. My style was anything but. I loved Prada and Donna Karan, as well as vintage and consignment kitsch. (People can and have accused me of many things but never of being a frump.) To Larry's credit, as radical as I turned in my fashion choices over the years, he never questioned my look or criticized my attire. I could put together some, uh, very interesting outfits. (When I said "hostess tiara" I meant just that.) One day, I decided to wear a long gown and tennis shoes to a fancy dinner. He simply smiled and shook his head. I loved that he let me be me, at least to a certain point.

So I combined my interest in kitsch, couture and a flair for the aesthetic with my love of the game, and decided to design something that average women could wear that wasn't quite so, well, bourgeois. I did some research and found a person who designed and manufactured ladies' cycling apparel. I loved her bike wear and she loved my golf designs so we formed a company called CareWear. The name was chosen to depict more than just a women's fashion line. I wanted to highlight the importance of a mission/passion behind a brand, a continuation of the Kids at Heart theme of heart-centered service and products. We decided that a portion of the proceeds from CareWear should go to women's mental health research (a near-and-dear cause) through the American Psychiatric Association. The hangtags on the clothes offered self-esteem-building tips for women with an 800 help line for those in distress. The clothing line itself, called Five

Easy Pieces, showcased Jetsons-inspired future wear for the busy female/golfer: a Coolmax top, micro-fiber skirt, vest, shorts and a unique accessory holder that I designed to Velcro onto a pocket to hold several tees, a ball marker, scorecard and pencil.

Once again (like many inventors), I was slightly ahead of a curve with my idea to be fashion-forward on the golf course. Back then, ladies didn't really want to draw attention to themselves on the course. They were just pleased to finally be allowed to play at private clubs and gain recognition in membership circles. It took a while for them (and me!) to be recognized as equal partners in the golf cart. And at that time, Coolmax (or, breathable micro-fiber fabrics) weren't being used at all in the golf industry. It was a totally new look. We blended golf attire with the latest in cycling fashion. We coined the phrase "blended dressing" because our Five Easy Pieces could be worn on the golf course AND look smart for trips to the grocery store, shopping mall or gal-pal visits . . . and even for cocktail hour at a neighborhood restaurant. I felt that people's lives were becoming increasingly busy. If we could wear sports clothing that could easily blend from one afternoon event to the next, and support a female-oriented nonprofit, it would be a match made in heaven. Voila! Blended dressing! My marketing noggin and fondness for collaboration came to the fore—as well as to the Fore! I approached the owners of Tambellini's, a successful, long-lived restaurant group in the Pittsburgh area. I asked them to team up with us to private-label bottles of their popular Italian salad dressing. On each bottle would be a Blended Dressing label. Not only would consumers look great on and off the green, they'd also get a great bottle of classic Italian dressing for their salad greens!

With an eye on selling the CareWear line to a larger clothing label, we spent six months in negotiation talks with a China-based clothing manufacturer. They were very interested in our line and we traveled back and forth from Pittsburgh to Los Angeles for meetings. Ultimately, though, their interest waned and my partner, Cathy, needed to put her focus back on her cycling apparel company. I spent the next several months with the clothes in the back of my car, driving across the state of Florida to golf shops, meeting with buyers at Saks Fifth Avenue in New York, and neighborhood pro shops. Although I did snag orders and sales were decent for a while, it seemed that the market wasn't ready for Judy Jetson on the golf course. Larry's reaction was supportive and mirrored mine in that he finally felt it might be time to cut our losses and enjoy wearing the sample line of size 8 clothing myself when I played golf. Nevertheless, those were fun, exciting times. I learned a great deal about clothing design, manufacturing and the intricacies of writing yet another business plan. Now, I am happy to see that many of the current golf clothes for women are hip and fashionable. Just look at Anna Kournikova and Annika Sorenstam! Perhaps it takes a celebrity athlete to endorse a radical new style and set the trend. And I still don my own CareWear fashions from time to time on the course—they've lasted all these years because we made them to be durable!

Over the next five years, Larry divested himself of all of his holdings and we decided to spend our winters in West Palm Beach, Florida. I was not totally sold on leading a retired life, yet I was willing to give it a whirl alongside Larry, while still intending to keep myself busy with entrepreneurial and spiritual pursuits. Feeling drawn to make my winters down south amount

Get into the habit of keeping a journal.

to more than just golf with the ladies, I began to journal my thoughts on personal development. Like everything else I had done, this ultimately morphed into a desire to share these thoughts with others. So, next on my invention assembly line was Mind Candy, a box of 31 daily affirmation cards based on my daily journal entries. Each card featured an inspirational phrase and a few words of wisdom about it. I wrote the wording and hired a graphic-designer to illustrate them. It was a simple, fun tool for self-transformation. To feed the body as well as the mind and soul, the box included a bag of colorful candy mints. The finished package looked like a candy bar with foil paper and a rainbow-colored brain on the wrapper. The tagline was: Mind Candy, A Real Head Trip! Mind Candy went on to sell at bookstores in Pennsylvania and Florida. At one point, Larry and I converted the living room of our West Palm Beach home into a Mind Candy factory. He was a big help. He would help stuff mint bags, label plastic containers and wrap foil around the boxes while watching his beloved Vanna White on Wheel of Fortune. In those years, tarot and other card decks were tucked behind the check-out counters of bookstores like cigarettes. They weren't

Use affirmation cards, or better yet, create your own.

big sellers—yet. Today, inspirational cards command their own shelves in the self-help sections of mainstream bookstores. I saw that trend coming and thought Mind Candy would be a tasty selection alongside the early offerings of Louise Hay, Doreen Virtue and other authors. I was pleased to get reorders from many of the retail stores that carried Mind Candy. And then, after a period of a year or so, I sadly realized that I couldn't devote the proper amount of time to this project because of the escalating attention Larry required from me. By then, his retirement was in full swing and he wanted to go, go, go. Yoga and massage classes, hosting lavish parties and travel were on his docket.

Truth was Larry always humored my business ventures—until they started to take off. Whenever any of my projects began to dip into our personal life of travel and leisure, he'd put his foot down. It was frustrating for me, as my sense of self was still in the blossoming stage. It wasn't that Larry didn't want me to have interests; he just didn't want them to interfere with my time with him. From a business standpoint, Larry loved that he could talk with me about my own business interests. But the moment one of my ideas started taking off, suddenly Larry would start having issues with it. According to my friend Deb, who had known Larry for a long time, it was because deep down Larry always knew (and perhaps feared) that I was going to be successful.

While in Florida, a golf buddy of mine, Jane, invited me to attend a new class at a bookstore where I had offered Mind Candy workshops a year prior. I didn't know it at the time, but I was about to attend a workshop that would impact the course of my life. It was entitled "Clear Your Clutter, Change Your Life!" And boy, oh boy, did my life change! Those classes not only gave me a rich knowledge base about Feng Shui, or, the ancient art of Oriental design, it also set the stage for finding my inner voice—and, more poignantly, the eventual dissolution of my marriage.

Once I began clearing my clutter and learning even more about empowerment through the ancient art of space design, I felt as though I had awakened from a long, lazy nap. Judy was finally back in Kansas after relocating her ruby slippers. I longed for more experiences of self-discovery. The next summer in Pittsburgh, I spent months cleaning out old files, pitching unused items, donating clothing and doing lots of thinking. In the midst of the rubble, I began to sense an emerging freedom and surety of self. Larry didn't know what to make of this. No, it wasn't my clothing choices he started to object to, it was something much more serious. I had

Feng Shui is another powerful tool that can be harnessed to bring about changes in your life.

begun to find my voice for the first time as a mature woman. And what happens when a woman's voice gives rise to inner desires that don't require a husband's approval? I bet many of you women know exactly what I am talking about.

I became less and less interested in our constant social whirl and the surface conversations that typically ensued. Larry wanted to party with larger and larger groups of people that I didn't know. I wanted to spend time in silence and on spiritual pursuits. I didn't blame him for my disinterest in our lifestyle or expect him to follow me. He had earned the right to live the life that suited him… But so had I. It became more and more obvious that Larry and I were growing apart, and talking about it amongst ourselves or with a counselor did nothing to erase the growing gap.

In order to get my certification in Feng Shui, I had to go to New York for training. I was proud the day I graduated from Feng Shui class as a master in 4th Stage Black Sect Tibetan Tantric Buddhist Feng Shui. I knew that I could build a respectable business as a consultant helping others redesign their spaces to support their intentions for a life of health, wealth and good fortune. As I began to implement my ideas, Larry quietly resented that they took my focus away from him.

"Where are my glasses?" he'd say, "Where are my shoes? Can we have lunch now? We're going to West Palm next week, okay?"

Larry had always been a high maintenance husband, and for many years I was more than happy to help him accomplish whatever he needed to. But now it was time for me to focus on me. It became increasingly difficult for me to manage his life and my own. Don't get me wrong, it was a wonderful lifestyle. We had traveled to Europe, the West Coast and wine country. We had enjoyed exciting shopping sprees in New York City, and vacations to places in and around the country. And with the spiritual understanding that we create our own reality, I can see now that I had participated in making Larry dependent on me. He was very needy of me in many ways, and I probably picked him out on some subconscious level because of my own desire to be needed and loved. Of course I had enjoyed our jet-set lifestyle—who wouldn't? But, more importantly, I had just wanted to be needed, to be loved, and to feel safe. Larry provided all that and much more.

Along with age and experience comes the knowledge that we enter into unspoken contracts in our lives until our truths change, and then we go our separate ways. My contract with Larry was coming to a close on many levels. We had shared an enormous amount of love, good times and personal growth. He had afforded me a wonderful life, and having been brought up to believe that a woman tended to the home and her husband's needs, I had done the same for him. But now I was beginning to feel that while I could still do this, I was also capable of so much more.

It wasn't Larry's age that became the issue, nor had it ever been. It simply became clear in the last years of our marriage that I was growing in ways that no longer allowed me to settle for anything less than I truly deserved. I deserved to live my days and nights in ways that nourished my soul, not weakened my spirit. And it wasn't Larry that I sought a divorce from—it was our lifestyle. He wasn't willing to compromise on his life of luxury and social glamour. I didn't expect him to. I simply expected me to speak up for what I wanted and I finally did. Larry didn't see things the way I did and wasn't willing to, so we decided to separate. As fate would have it, around that same time, my Feng Shui partner, Janet Cam, and I landed a cushy contract with Bloomingdale's in Washington, DC. They hired us to conduct regular Feng Shui seminars in their house-wares department. It gave me something decent and real to focus on—something that was all mine, and all me.

Looking back, I can see how all the different aspects of my life had woven together to prepare me for what was yet to come. Throughout my married years, even with my focus on husband, home and family, I had kept a big toe in business through CareWear, Mind Candy and Feng Shui consulting—all projects that I loved. I learned that I could nurture children with the true soul of a mother, keep par with business people on the golf course, and win hands down in social graces and party planning as hostess for a multitude of gatherings. Larry gave me a firm sense of business savvy by watching him in action and offering me a safety net to try out new ideas. Many of his friends were CEOs of companies, heads of educational institutions and respected politicians. Just like in high school, I was friends with everybody and able to get along with all kinds. In Larry's circles, I fine-tuned these abilities until they became second nature, which translates to an invaluable asset in the business arena.

I would need this ability more than ever in the 18 months to come. If being Larry's wife was my apprenticeship in business, my next undertaking—this one unexpected and with Larry's full consent—would be my MBA and PhD combined.

7.

Greasy Fries and a PhD

If God were to say, "Okay, Judy, you're telling me you want to run a business and you want to do it now, so I'm going to give you the fastest, most effective trial-by-fire way to learn everything you need to know," would I have imagined THIS?

Spiritual wisdom suggests we always have a choice, no matter what circumstances we face. With what was to come in the next phase of my life, my two options appeared to be: jump into the frying vat or face financial ruin. For good measure, a pop quiz on emotional fortitude was thrown into the mix. Recently separated from Larry, I would be earning my in-the-trenches MBA on my own and, in the process, would watch this man whom I still loved mentally deteriorate. "And let's not leave out the physical aspect," God could have added. "While doing all of this alone, Judy, your body will be in constant pain with a health challenge, as well."

During the declining years of our marriage, Larry had pledged some of our investments as collateral for a business loan to an individual whose company's financial standing was already in arrears. When this individual defaulted on the loan, rather than lose the money he gave as collateral, Larry decided to invest triple that amount in hopes of recouping the monies. The investment was in a group of fast food restaurants that Larry knew nothing about: Steak Escape, Gloria Jean's Coffee and Arby's. Everyone had advised him against this—including his children, his trusted attorney and me. Larry had made many smart business and investment decisions over the span of his career; maybe this one was a function of "you win some, you lose some." When Larry signed the agreement to run these establishments, he essentially became partners with a man named Jerry, who he barely knew.

"You know the business," Larry said to him. "You run the companies. I'm going to Florida."

Larry and I had separated but remained good friends. He continued to winter in Florida. Janet and I were focused on our part-time work with Bloomingdale's. I got wind of this Jerry character through Larry and our legal advisor. He seemed unscrupulous. My instincts were confirmed when I discovered that Jerry had bounced a $100,000 check. *What else has he done?* I wondered.

Torn between my own blossoming career and the warning signs that Larry's sizable investment was in precarious hands, I said to him one day, "Larry, you don't know anything about this person you have in charge of these restaurants and you're living down there until the spring thaw. Why don't I just look in on things every so often? I don't know anything about the restaurant business but at least I can help oversee accountability issues." Larry agreed. So I fulfilled whatever Feng Shui consulting contracts and public speaking engagements I had scheduled and then put everything else on temporary hold.

My short-term goal with the restaurants was to learn as much as I could as quickly as possible to enable me temporarily to oversee the company on Larry's behalf. In order to effectively do so, I took the initiative to get training in the essentials of the fast food industry in general, and in these three food businesses in particular. First gig: Arby's corporate training in central Florida—smack in the thick of the summer heat and humidity. For weeks, I worked alongside the cooks learning how to slice paper-thin roast beef and douse French fries in boiling-hot oil. Talk about the antipode to my espoused lifestyle! I transgressed from a holistic, health-conscious system of juicing and eating mostly fresh, organic food to subsisting in a saturated-fat pit and everything that involved—including an eruption of facial acne from soaking up cooking grease, and a lazy habit of reaching for caffeine-loaded diet soft drinks to quench my constant thirst. Around this time, a dull pain in my hips that had been niggling at me for a while suddenly worsened. Both hip sockets now ached from standing on hard flooring for double-shifts waiting on customers, as well as spending long hours learning the ropes at warp speed. As weeks went on, the pain intensified to the point where I had difficulty walking.

But I couldn't walk away from the situation. The more involved I became with the businesses, the more I noticed things that weren't copasetic—thousands of dollars of theft by employees, failing morale, sliding food and operational quality, and bad vibes amongst the vendors and corporate franchise staff. I had no choice but to shift my attention to stopping the company's internal bleeding and getting operations back on an even keel.

So I jumped from the frying vat into the fire. I delved more deeply into understanding the money flow, labor costs and food percentages, and how they compared to other fast food numbers in the industry. In doing so, I learned that many vendors hadn't been paid and consequently had placed the former owner on a cash-on-delivery accounting status, which put our cash flow in jeopardy. Franchise fees were overdue and the books had been cooked to keep royalties lower than they should have been. Then I discovered more information about our dear Jerry that would soon put the company in a real pickle. Not only had he not been making deposits and paying taxes; he was also under indictment for continuing to represent himself as a CPA after his license had been revoked. Big gulp! Larry's general manager was a felon!

I informed Larry about all of this and we made a joint decision to fire Jerry from his general manager position. With Jerry's departure, there was no one to run the five businesses. So I offered to go to work as Larry's partner—which was, in a sense, a kiss of death because my name was now on all legal documents.

For better or worse, I signed on and was immediately in charge of 60 employees—from fry cooks and cashiers to regional managers and franchise field reps. One thing I'd noticed from the very beginning and could no longer ignore was that many of our employees seemed wounded emotionally and psychologically. They rarely looked me in the eyes when we spoke, often glanced at me with distrust and clung to cynicism, vulgarities and negative gossip. This did nothing for my confidence, of course, but before anything else could be accomplished, I needed to be sure I could trust at least some people . . . and them me. So I did what I could to both earn and gain the trust of whomever I could in order to collectively move forward with improving on-the-job conditions.

My mind kept coming back to the franchisor-franchisee situation. The whole underlying structure of the arrangement seemed shaky to me. I started to get this vibe during my owner-operator training about the negative aspects of how the franchisor and their franchisee's relate to one another. Historically, franchisor-franchisee relations seemed to be less than supportive or trustworthy. Policing tactics and surprise visits to stores by company execs seemed to put the franchisees on edge, never knowing who would show up when, and for what reason. Franchisees wanting to cut costs and increase profits by supplying customers with inferior products went strictly against company policy, which led to guerilla response tactics by corporate. It was a vicious cycle that I believed could have been avoided with better communication and creative negotiation on both sides. I was interested to explore how this could instead be a simple win-win situation. The franchisee learns the business from the franchisor, complies with the regulations of the industry and everybody makes money. It seemed like an easy-to-follow, tried-and-true formula.

One day while talking to the upper execs at Arby's, I suggested, "Hey guys, let's work together on this." They looked at me like I had three heads. Their reaction may have been one part due to my naïveté and one part due to their growing mistrust from Jerry's nefarious business tactics. In my eyes, there was a third part. Like many executives in the higher echelons, they often viewed those lower on the food chain solely according to how they impacted the monthly numbers and investor's ROI, as opposed to seeing them as real people with real feelings, mostly unmet needs and poor communication and social skills. With my focus squarely on my own learning curve, however, I was hardly in a position to suggest any enlightened communication or behavior methodologies. Still, it became embedded in my mind that there was fertile ground to be tilled in the future with respect to nurturing human kindness that reflects an interconnectedness amongst us all—from top execs to fry cooks.

> ✄ *Nurture human kindness—with everyone, regardless of their status in life or their role in any organization.*

In retrospect, I hadn't known the managers and employees long enough to develop any real confidence in their level of loyalty or even understand the industry enough to gain any respect in their eyes. These people had been doing their jobs for years and I had been learning the business for less than a year. *Who did I think I was* to go in there and tell them how to do their jobs better? But I just knew there *had* to be a better way than the current environment of rampant theft, mistrust and cynical attitudes on life in general. I would have to figure this out my own way, beginning as I typically do—from the inside out. A possible solution arose from asking myself the questions:

How could I help these people? How could I best serve them?

For me, an overriding concern was that franchisor-franchisee relationship—particularly, how the franchise owners treated their own employees.

🦋 *Cultivate an attitude of service to others. Rather than thinking of what others can do for you, start thinking about how you can best serve them.*

These people were living in fear. A lot of them stole from us. Most were never acknowledged. After contemplating all of this, I came up with an idea to raise the level of morale, build a team of committed staff and add something positive to their lives and mindset. It was in our contract as a franchisee to construct a renovation of our Arby's every five years to refurbish the look. I engaged an architect to draw up blueprints. While under construction, I planned to bring all of our employees to a central site and offer specialized training in conflict resolution, motivational behavior and self-esteem building, among other topics. I lined up executive coaches, speakers on abundance mindset, yoga instructors and other professionals. When I announced this agenda to the employees, they were thrilled beyond belief. Almost overnight, their attitudes improved. They couldn't wait to attend this training.

"No employer or franchise owner has ever cared so much about us as individuals," one of our location managers said to me one day.

This opened a deep conversation among the employee group and me. What I found was that they had important things they wanted to say, and they wanted to be heard. I listened closely and came away with the strong sense that while a paycheck was very important to them, what I was proposing to offer was even more so. I wanted to give them life skills that they could take with them and use for the rest of their lives. Well balanced, appreciated employees would work better and be more engaged in their jobs, I reasoned. I felt good about the upcoming training and everything was scheduled to begin on September 15, 2001.

Then, 9/11 happened. Because three of the five restaurants were located at the Greater Pittsburgh International Airport, all of which were ailing when we took them over, we took an unrecoverable hit. With no one other than ticketed passengers allowed through security into the main retail area of the terminal, the airport became desolate. I couldn't deny that we were going under, and fast. All renovations were ceased. We closed the restaurants and legally declared Chapter 11.

And I couldn't deny anymore that I could barely walk. Some mind-body experts say that hip problems symbolize an inability to move forward on one's proper life path. Others have suggested to me that because

I was unable or unwilling to fully express my creative self during my adult years—something that is vitally important to me—those energies became stuck in the same area of the body where women bear children. My natural inclination to birth my creations was stunted during my married years. When I had begun to feel unsteady in my marriage about four years prior, my hips had become my sore spot. I had allowed my circumstances to thwart my passion to somehow make a difference in the world. And now my body was screaming at me to do something about it. What a concept!

It made so much sense. Before year end, I was in the hospital, undergoing surgery to replace my left hip; suddenly, I was forced to focus on my own needs—something that had become foreign to me. (It is, however, something that I'm learning is essential to one's well being and sense of empowerment. We must take care of ourselves in order to be of any good to others.)

As flight attendants say: "When you put on your own oxygen mask first, you're better equipped to assist others."

As I thought through my own needs, it occurred to me that while there were many reasons behind my decision to leave Larry, the most compelling one was that I'd finally found my voice and it no longer matched the words that Larry wanted to hear.

In the meantime, while I was working through my decision to leave, legal hearings had begun with Larry's eldest son stepping in with power of attorney. I walked gingerly into many bankruptcy meetings with my cane and a renewed sense of determination to see things confidently through to the bitter end. Larry Jr. and I worked together to steer the company through Chapter 11 while Larry remained mostly in Florida. I was left to deal with the district attorneys, executives of all the franchisors, the employees and my managers, and I watched as various people came out of the woodwork to take advantage of our misfortune. There were restaurant developers who saw an opportunity to buy us out for pennies on the dollar, neighborhood attorneys and so-called friends who seemed to delight in Larry's financial downturn, and dishonest employees who used the chaos and confusion of 9/11 to further their own financial self-interests by stealing product inventory and money bags on their way to the night bank depository.

But the biggest emotional toll on me at that time was facing the truth that Larry's mental health had begun to seriously decline. We spoke regularly and our conversations became increasingly disjointed as his failing mental state grew more pronounced. I still cared about him deeply and felt sad that he was no longer my partner, my husband, my love. He gradually became my child, who I wanted to protect. His mental swiftness had softened into the gauze-filtered gaze of an aging loved one. He seemed to quickly change from a vital, smart, clever man to a confused, fragile, dependent being. With the financial chaos swirling around me, and my own failing health, I simply had no extra emotional support to lend anyone. Larry wasn't able to give emotional comfort to me, either. Even though I had friends and family members for conversation or a shoulder to cry on, I found that, ultimately, I only had myself to rely on.

In the end, we sold the company, lost millions and were left with federal authorities questioning why our accountant had never paid sales and payroll taxes. It took years to resolve and pay off the debt.

Would I have chosen to go through all this? Absolutely not. But when I think about that intense 18-month period, I don't know how else I could have learned business in such a thorough, accelerated way. It was my real-life doctorate. With my financial future at stake, that added element of survival had simply brought a greater urgency to it all. I learned so much in a short span of time—not just about business but personally. More than ever, I knew that I was a supporter of workers' rights, freedom and personal voice. I became even more committed to a values-and integrity-driven business model, and I left the whole experience determined to create one if given the chance.

On a personal level, my greatest lesson was to continue to honor my internal guidance system and to trust the supreme correctness of the universe that everything always unfolds perfectly—no matter what outward appearances show.

So, yes, I believe that there's always a higher purpose if we take the time to look for it. And every experience, no matter how difficult, contains a gift that, if we pay attention to it, will serve us well in the future. I would continue to learn this truth to greater and grander degrees in the immediate years to follow. Those would be the most challenging years of my life to date, for reasons both seen and unseen.

8.

Turning Point: Go West

Epiphanies can happen so innocently, and when you least expect them. There I was, just sitting at a traffic light in Pittsburgh in October 2002. As if scripted for a TV movie, I was literally at a crossroads, uncertain about the next right steps in my life. Those past few years had been far from joyful. Divorce, bankruptcy and major surgery had left me feeling vulnerable, stunted, waiting for a green light of sorts.

Just then, an amazing sensation rushed over me. Sitting in my SUV, I knew in an instant that an incredibly important movement was happening in the world and I needed to be a part of it. I didn't know where or how, but I knew why. I still felt an internal calling, something I needed to explore. Perhaps the concept behind my first attempt at this deep sense of vocation, my business "failure," had simply been ahead of its time. Now, finally, I was ready to make a right turn towards my destiny. The pull was so strong that within a few months I'd packed all my belongings in that same vehicle, said goodbye to family, lifelong friends and the town I'd known forever, and set the GPS for due west—my best hunch of where this "movement" was occurring.

And while this internal nudge to relocate to the west coast was powerful, for good measure, the universe threw in an added incentive to ensure that I would follow through on it.

Four months earlier, during my first ever course at the Chopra Center (more about that in a moment), I had met a man who seemed like the perfect match for me. George was young, handsome, kindhearted, spiritual, athletic, business oriented and on the board of a well-known spiritually minded foundation. He even wore Prada and wrote me poetry; how could I not be smitten? Before long, George was talking about us being together and moving to San Diego. As I got to know him better, however, subtle cues started to present themselves that indicated some possible imbalances in his personality. For instance, he spoke freely and frequently about having suffered intense abuse in his childhood. I listened with an open heart even when he went into what seemed to be too much graphic detail about situations in his past. Then, as the weeks went by, his inner rage seemed to escalate to the point where I actually became frightened to be in his presence. In one instance, while in his car and for no apparent reason, George suddenly started to drive so fast I began to fear for my safety. That was when I knew that literally and figuratively, I needed to hit the brakes. In the end, it just wasn't meant to be… or perhaps it was? For by then, I had relocated to San Diego for an even more important reason: to define my life's work and finally get down to the business of accomplishing it.

One of my intentions upon relocating to California was to become part of a spiritually likeminded community. Coincidentally, a friend of a friend had told me about a tiny, one-room apartment that was available for sublease at the La Costa Golf Resort for a pittance. I didn't know how long I'd be able to afford living there, or where else I could go at that point, as I hadn't yet gotten my geographic bearings and didn't know anyone in California. Financially, I had a small monthly alimony agreement that was to last for less than a year; beyond that, I had no idea what I'd be doing to earn a living. As I saw it, my best option was to simply trust and go with what was being presented to me at the time. In this case, it was a comfortable and quite beautiful place to temporarily call home.

Beach prayer

So, there I was, living at La Costa—a beautiful place—and there was no denying the weather in San Diego was gorgeous, as well. At the same time, however, the feelings of hope and excitement that had pulled me there still hadn't resulted in anything concrete. Very soon, the holidays were upon me, and reality set in; I have to admit that spending Christmas on my own, with no one to share a traditional eggnog, left me feeling intensely lonely and sorry for myself. I was in a strange new place, with none of my friends close by, and nothing familiar to engage me that would help pass the time. The hardest thing to cope with was the knowledge that there was no one in San Diego who really cared about me. I tried to make friends with people in my building, but a lot of them were retired, with lives and families of their own. With no support network to wrap myself up in, I felt naked, vulnerable and raw with emotion.

For years, I'd been in partial hibernation, at least from my true self. Like waves under the ocean's surface, I knew I was gathering momentum for something as yet unseen that was going to require my full attention. Something big was coming down the pipeline, I was certain of it. And once that wave hit the shore, I would be ready to dive in and play... but in the meantime... gee, if only I had someone to talk to.

God, please show me why I am here in California, I'd often pray. *I know there has to be a reason.* The only thing I was certain of was that, on some deep level, I had been preparing for something my entire life. All I had was a deep conviction that there was an important movement afoot and that I needed to be part of it.

Weeks earlier, reinventing my life had seemed exciting, adventurous, exotic even. Now I wasn't so convinced. In Pittsburgh, at least I had credibility in the community, respect from peers, familiar neighborhood haunts to make me feel welcome, and social and business networks to rely upon. In southern California, where I didn't know a soul, it was more like "Who the hell are you?"

For the first time in my life, I was completely alone. And while I knew that there was an upside to this situation in that my options were now as vast as the shoreline, somehow it didn't quite assuage the intense loneliness that welled up inside me.

Many days I would make my way down to the beach, kick off my sandals, and with only the sea for inspiration I'd make phone calls about possible job opportunities and strategize on paper about the kind of work I wanted to find. And pray...

Oh, I prayed a lot those early days in San Diego.

God, please tell me, show me...what do YOU want me to do for the rest of my life? I would frequently ask.

The desire to be of service, to aid humanity in a powerful and positive way, still bellowed in my bones. On some level, I was still inwardly devastated that my Kids at Heart venture hadn't taken off in the way I had always known it had the potential to. Over the years, I'd pushed that disappointment into the recesses of my mind. But now I realized it still echoed in my heart.

On another level entirely, I also had the feeling that I was simply marking time; waiting for something just as special and unique as Kids at Heart to ignite the spark of creativity in me again.

In the meantime, my money was fast running out.

Please, God, reveal my destiny. I promise I'm ready. And please could you make it quick because I really need to make a living!

The Chopra course that Jen and I had attended four months earlier delved into the *Seven Spiritual Laws of Success*. In his book of the same name, Deepak defines success in life as "the continued expansion of happiness and the progressive realization of worthy goals." Such success, he goes on to write, is the result of tapping into the "field of all possibilities," as well as understanding the principles behind "attention" and "intention"—all things that I had been experimenting with on my own for years. As Deepak explains, "Intention organizes its own fulfillment" because it transforms and organizes energy and information to bring about desired outcomes. We see the expression of this infinite organizing power in everything that is alive—from a blade of grass to every cell of our body.

While I had been experimenting with aspects of these universal laws for some time, Deepak's elegant and profound articulation of them seemed to diffuse through me to a superfine degree. I had relied on the power of intention-setting to steer me through various situations in my adult life. Now I wanted to up the ante. I would experiment with the "organizing power of the universe" in every *aspect* of my life. Not just with vital matters such as livelihood and relationships but with everyday practical matters too.

The irony of my temporary living situation at a world-renowned luxury resort was not lost on me. There I was, at least from outward appearances, ensconced in the very same lifestyle that had become so tiresome and unfulfilling to me. How interesting that now here I was back in a similar place to that which I had just escaped—albeit with two fundamental exceptions: one was money (of which I now had very little), and the other was that, despite the wealth around me, this particular environment had the spiritual overtones that I'd been seeking. All I wanted was to dedicate myself to finding my true path, and Spirit had seen fit to put me back into a similar milieu from that which I had just escaped. I pondered the reason for this as I watched golfers in crisp, white slacks and skirts tee off across the manicured greens. Was this some cosmic test to see how serious I was? A test to gauge whether I could resist falling back into my former, cushioned, ladies-that-lunch-and-play-golf lifestyle? Not that I could afford to do so even if I had wanted to.

Then it hit me one day while observing a group of tanned, toned and diamond-studded women lunching near the lawn. Although I was surrounded by all the trappings of my old lifestyle at La Costa, I wasn't really a part of it. Instead, I was being given an opportunity to view it from the outside looking in. Part of what I saw was seekers with good intentions and high credit lines. It reinforced for me that all we really need is the "good intent" part, and that none of us can buy our way into spiritual awareness, no matter how materially wealthy we are, if we don't have that authentic underpinning. I had embarked on this adventure out west because I had a different belief about what constitutes "the good life." Material riches can be wonderful but what's the point if you feel empty inside? I yearned for a full connection to my spiritual core and the discovery of my life purpose. Everyone has access to this for themselves, if desired—young or old, wealthy or poor. It had taken me a long time to discover it, but now finally, at the age of 47, I was free to pursue this personal desire.

For the time being, I felt safe at La Costa, surrounded by spiritually-minded others. Months earlier, while planning my exit strategy out west, I'd written some very detailed intentions on large sheets of paper about the lifestyle I wanted to create in California. At the time, many of the details had seemed far-fetched, like shooting for the moon. But with Deepak's "quantum field of infinite possibility" fresh in my mind, I had seen no need to limit my thinking. Upon moving into my tiny quarters at La Costa, I'd rolled and tucked those sheets of paper under my bed, where they lay forgotten until months later while on a phone call with Jennifer.

Always write your intentions down and keep them for future reference.

"Didn't you write some intentions a while back about your personal, spiritual and career aspirations?" she reminded me.

"I did."

"Can you find them and read them to me?" she asked.

I reached under the bed, pulled out the sheets, and recited a handful of my intentions to Jen. Then I came to this one:

I INTEND THIS OR SOMETHING BETTER: *To live amidst the beauty of nature, near the beach, within walking distance to a gym where I can keep up my personal commitment to exercising and eating healthy food, also within walking distance to a spiritual community of people who meditate and practice yoga, and access to an inexpensive driver who knows the area and can safely transport me to appointments until I get my bearings.*

"Oh . . . my . . ." I trailed off mid-sentence.

Lulled by the hum of a lawnmower outside my window, a chain of mini-realizations rattled through my mind like dominoes. Walking towards the window with the phone to my ear, I began to describe to Jennifer the beautifully landscaped gardens and ornate fountain that marks the entrance to La Costa Resort and Spa. I had walked by this sight every day for the past several months as I came and went from my third-floor apartment. My view overlooked the resort's spacious pool area and legendary golf course—which I passed on my short walk to the gym.

I was already living the dream I had envisioned and I hadn't even realized it.

I joked with friends back home that I used the resort lobby as my office. I pretended that the fireplace area was my spacious living room with tasteful, classic artwork adorning the walls. Many evenings, I would enjoy a glass of wine and appetizer in front of the fireplace, or lounge in overstuffed chairs as I settled into my Sunday ritual of reading the *New York Times* with a *venti latte*. My "room with a view" was literally a nine-iron shot away with a well-traveled, brightly lit path in between.

I was like the children's storybook character Eloise, living at the hotel amidst its beauty. The maintenance crew and valet guys (my personal drivers) were all my pals, as were the employees of the Chopra Center, which housed a meditation room and yoga studio. I had free access to the state-of-the-art La Costa gym and became fast friends with a guy who worked as a trainer. Toli had the chiseled face and body of a Greek god, and a spiritual maturity that more than matched his physical strength. As we lifted weights, boxed and did calisthenics with an exercise ball, we'd chat about self-improvement, not just of the body, but also of the mind and spirit. Oh, those soulful eyes, that Greek accent . . . it was a painless (and cost free) way to get in shape.

"It's no mistake that you landed at La Costa," Jennifer exclaimed, astonished by everything I told her. "You literally manifested your intention!"

It was true, with just one exception. Back in Pittsburgh when I had written those words, I had assumed that the only way to enjoy these accoutrements was through owning them. I hadn't considered that I could enjoy all this without the responsibility of buying, maintaining and paying taxes on it. My rent was inexpensive and the amenities were free. The universe had managed to bring me everything on my wish list and more—and blessedly under budget, too!

Relating all this to Jennifer, I was gob-smacked. I had witnessed miracles in the process of intending one's wishes before but this was right under my nose. How could I have missed the obvious? When we hung up, I immediately walked to my meditation corner and spent the next half hour in a state of deep gratitude.

As it turns out, being at La Costa played a role in materializing more than just my living quarters. With only a notion of the kind of work I wanted to become involved in, my first thought was to knock on the doors of the Chopra Center and ask if they needed help with

Create a gratitude journal, and get into the habit of focusing on, and writing down, all the things that happened during the day that you are grateful for.

marketing. Because of Deepak's celebrity status, hundreds of people wanted to be in his inner circle. I didn't have a typical résumé to give the COO, since I'd mostly worked as an entrepreneur, developing and promoting my own ideas. (To this day, my business strength lies in the fact that I love to market, promote and innovate.) I knew that I could add value to an organization that stood for something I believed in—particularly personal empowerment, a long-term interest of mine. The marketing staff was open to hearing what I had to suggest so I made presentation after presentation after presentation. At times, I felt like a back alley hustler with an oversized raincoat stuffed with stolen goods.

"I've got this great watch. Oh, okay, you don't want that? How about this, it's just your size? No? Okay, then how about if I give you a discount and throw in this item that I just happen to have on special today?"

I gave every sales pitch known to man—as well as a few that likely weren't. Finally, and probably because they felt sorry for me, they gave me a chance. That's all I had really wanted, a chance. I started off doing meager marketing and public relations work, and was compensated in educational barter dollars—which was okay with me for the time being. I was able to attend many uplifting seminars that proved to be extremely helpful as I navigated the emotionally choppy waters of setting up a new existence 3,000 miles from home. At the same time, I plugged away at starting a website for women called YinRising.com. This endeavor didn't feel quite right to me but I explored what I might contribute to the burgeoning on-line population of women business owners who also wanted to do something meaningful in the world.

Reflecting on this period of time, I think about what it takes, emotionally and psychologically, to leap the chasm from whatever current situation we may find ourselves in to the higher ground of a deeply felt vocation. How do we leave a dead-end job, a career we loathe, an industry that challenges our values, or from being a stay-at-home parent into an already over-crowded workforce that isn't exactly waiting to embrace what we will have to offer? When we look within and do whatever personal work is required to determine our heartfelt sense of purpose, the stakes become higher because we are more emotionally invested in our endeavors. If our chosen work is entrepreneurial in nature, we must deal with rejection, often repeatedly, from those who don't resonate with or understand our creations. The question "who do you think you are?" is posed more frequently, either in words or raised eyebrows.

At times when I've jumped into the void, the process of intention-setting has helped me get from here to there. Even if we don't know what we want, it brings to the fore a trail of clues that lead to at least a partial answer. Humbling myself in front of the Chopra marketing staff and vying to make a contribution there felt right because, based on the intentions I'd set, I was certain that something good would come of it. (As you will discover in the next chapter, what eventually came of it was far grander than anything I could have imagined at the time.) When our goals begin to formulate from a more authentic, inner place and we become engaged in the act of bringing them into manifestation, a momentum takes hold. And as we continue to refine what we want and who we want to become, our intentions become more refined, as well.

🦋 *Remember—there are hidden gifts in every experience. Accept and cultivate gratitude for what is, and then set your intentions for change.*

In the meantime, what I've learned about the process is this: we have to sit in the job we're in, the life we're in, the relationship we're in, or whatever the situation may be, and first get to a place of gratitude by saying *"where I am right now is the perfect place to be. I'm thankful for the experience. I'm thankful for the learning AND by the way, dear God, here are my intentions."* For many years,—and this is a big one for me—I wanted to be "over there." I didn't want to be in the situation I was in, even though I know now that it was all for a valuable reason. When I reached a level of acceptance wherein I was able to say, "Right here is exactly where I need to be, right in this job, right in this health crisis, right in this marital breakup, no regrets, no should-haves or could-haves," is when the synchronicities started to occur that led me down the right avenues toward where I am now. And the process continues every day.

As I continued to steep myself in life at La Costa—working part time at the Chopra Center and participating in educational seminars that helped me think through my next steps,—I kept up my ritual of walks to the ocean. Its beauty and permanence was a natural reminder that in a world of all possibilities, when we combine attention and intention, our heart's desires flow back to us in waves. In fact, one was about to knock me over in the most playful way.

9.

Eavesdropping on the Bus

SynchroDestiny . . . what a perfect name for the course I was about to take *and* for what was about to happen in my life. Jennifer and her husband, John, had decided to fly out and join me for this popular educational seminar at the Chopra Center a few months after I moved out west. I don't think I'd ever been so happy to see two loving and familiar faces as I was to see Jennifer and John.

Of course synchronicities happened that week. *Of course* I aligned more closely with my destiny. Uh, maybe that's why it's called SynchroDestiny. You see, it hadn't yet dawned on me that my reason for being in California was to create the next iteration of my Kids at Heart venture—the very first health club in the country for children. I'd stuffed that dream so far back into the corners of my mind that I hadn't thought of working on another children's program. Maybe I was afraid to hear myself say aloud that I still believed this was my soul's desire.

Maybe someone had to say it for me.

On the last day of the workshop, Jennifer, John and I were on a shuttle bus to a finale dinner in San Diego with Deepak and the other attendees. The evening was to be a celebration of our healing week. We were chatting away when, all of a sudden, I heard a woman say, clear as a bell and in my direction, as if speaking directly to me:

"Did you know the Chopra Center is looking to develop a children's program?"

The bus seemed to fall silent. The hair stood up on the back of my neck. The next few minutes passed in slow motion. I looked at Jennifer. She was looking at me, her eyes wide with amazement. She, too, had felt the magnitude of those words. Jen glanced over at the woman then back at me.

Dare I say something to her? I thought. I couldn't. I was speechless, as if I'd just been told about the Second Coming. That's what it felt like, a second coming, a second shot at my dream, another chance to get it right.

For the rest of the week, I rolled this over in my mind. *Do I emotionally have what it takes to go through that again? Do I want to risk my heart and soul again?* In practical terms, I knew I could do it. I could create an innovative children's program with the basis of the Kids at Heart business model, only supercharged and updated to reflect the lifestyle and mindset of the new millennium. When I pulled back the veil of disappointment I'd been feeling about Kids at Heart, I still had within me a passion to reinvent community-based children's centers that nurture, support and empower kids through compassionate, life-affirming activities. I couldn't deny that I felt exhilarated just thinking about the possibilities. My spirit was seduced all over again and, from that moment on, the idea wouldn't leave me alone.

I decided to test the waters by meeting for a casual lunch at La Costa Spa with the center's head educator and ayurvedic chef, Leanne Backer. She was a solid veteran of the human potential movement and one of the center's top-rung people. Leanne had chatted with me at many of the courses and often joined me in group meditation at the end of the day. We also rubbed elbows from time to time in the office when I was doing marketing work for the center. As I waited for Leanne to arrive at the *al fresco* dining room, I gazed beyond the hibiscus in full bloom at the perfectly sculpted 18-hole golf course. For a moment, I reflected on my previous married life. Back then, I was very fortunate to have opportunities to play golf and dine at country clubs. As much of a privilege as that was and as much as I love golf, I'd always had a sense that something crucial was missing. The yearning to live for a greater purpose and connect with other spiritually conscious individuals who were making a positive difference in the lives of others had remained unfulfilled inside me. Now here I was, in the hub of a spiritually vibrant community, having lunch near the greens again—only this time it was for a reason that felt real and true.

Over steaming lentil soup and a ginger drink chaser, I mentioned what I'd overheard on the bus then recounted my background in children's wellness programming. I pulled out some storyboards of the types of program innovations and roving curriculum I planned to offer, as well as a coloring book that I was producing with recipes, activities and games that reflected various New Thought principles. Leanne was so taken with the presentation that she offered to set up a meeting with the chief operating officer on her personal recommendation. She also readily agreed to have a sampling of recipes from her successful cookbook in my CosmiKids Fun Book for children.

I was thrilled at the possibility of being even peripherally aligned with an organization that stood for a lot of the things that were important to me. By then I'd had some time watching Deepak in a multitude of settings—in the gym, on the practice tee, in the boardroom, over luncheon meetings and leading his world-famous seminars. He was always friendly, concise and helpful. And he seemed to embrace a values and integrity-driven business model as the leader of an organization that empowers people. He appeared to integrate business and spirituality quite well, and I admired that.

Once I had the ear of the center's chief operating officer, I outlined how I would develop and implement a world-class children's program for them under several conditions: I would fund it myself and retain ownership/creative control, and I'd infuse the curriculum with enlightened philosophies and life-enhancing principles of many modern day great thinkers—not just Deepak, because my vision for building a conscious business model included collaboration and co-creation. Very soon, I would find myself happily aligning with Barbara Marx Hubbard, Don Beck, Lynn Twist, Dr. Masaru Emoto and Neale Donald Walsch, among other visionary New Thought leaders, teachers and authors. I had also been greatly inspired by the "integral education" philosophy and practices of Sri Aurobindo, one of India's greatest modern philosophers (1872—1950), and his spiritual partner, Mirra Alfassa (1878—1973), affectionately known as The Mother.

I explained to the COO how I'd merged inspiration from the Sri Aurobindo Center and other sources with my own. I understood (and agreed) that they needed a program for parents who wanted to experience the center's workshops but didn't want to leave their kids at home to do it. Many of these were spiritually-minded moms and dads who wanted to expose their little ones to the same holistic principles they were learning as adults—but in a kid-accessible kind of way. Far from babysitting, I imagined a full-bodied curriculum that made it possible for children to reap the same nurturing benefits their parents were simultaneously enjoying, such as an ability to go with the flow, increased confidence and self-esteem, a heightened ability to focus, being okay with how things are and less worry. The initial seven weeks of activities at the Chopra Camp for ages four and older would consist of the emerging philosophies and creations that I had accumulated and formulated to date, including (but not limited to) intuition training, expressive arts, yoga and breathwork, mindfulness practices, teachings of Mother Earth, multi-cultural rhythmic dance, aspects of healthy eating, and rest and reflection. These activities would help children gain a deeper knowledge of stress reduction, conflict resolution and personal empowerment skills, self-discovery tools and techniques, environmental awareness, an appreciation for healthy eating and food preparation, compassion training and ethnic diversity.

The COO listened carefully to my presentation and asked for time to take everything under advisement and get back to me.

I prayed for a positive outcome to this meeting yet, regardless, the rocket had been launched. The fire had been lit. The fat lady had sung. Any uncertainty about my dharma abruptly ended and I was brimming with ideas for creating an integrative, child-led experience like no other. Plenty had changed in the 20 years since I had first launched Kids at Heart. The world had changed. The way we educate our youth had changed. It seemed to me that schools and community-based children's programs were no longer enough for today's youth. Conversely, in some respects, they are too much: too much testing, too many restrictions, guidelines, rules and expectations. In the past few decades, our world seems to have shifted in so many ways— away from structure and into free-flowing, inclusive evolvement for everyone of all ages. It's been proven that children's IQs have risen dramatically. They simply need more. In their blossoming evolutionary maturity, they are looking for more sophisticated and meaningful experiences (and so are adults).

I had articulated much of this to the COO during our meeting. We spoke further by phone. After several weeks of negotiation, the Chopra Center gave me their answer.

"We'd like you to create and produce a premiere children's program at our center for an international audience. And we'd like it to launch in six months."

Six months? *Oh yes*, I thought, remembering what I'd practiced all week at SynchroDestiny and other workshops. With the quantum field of pure potentiality at my disposal to help orchestrate the fulfillment of my desire to pull this off, it could be done. *Of course* it could.

"You got it," I said.

Clearly, my intentions to be immersed in a spiritual community, to do business in a kinder, gentler way, and to make a difference in the world with cool, intelligent, likeminded others were becoming manifest. As my girlfriend Karynne Boese, a prominent lifestyle and recovery coach on the west coast says, the fulfillment of each intention is like a cosmic wink from the universe that all is as it should be, and that desires are on their way to being perfectly fulfilled—most times, even beyond our wildest dreams. Several months earlier, praying on the beach, could I have imagined that I'd be reinventing my Kids at Heart dream at a world renowned center for spiritual development that I personally admired and enjoyed? One thing's for sure, my prayers were being answered loud and clear. I felt the rightness of it all under my skin and in the center of my chest when that woman on the bus, my angel in disguise, delivered exactly the message that I was ready to hear.

Once more, everything that had occurred in those critical months seemed to be supremely orchestrated from above—my romance with George, landing at La Costa, being on that bus—because I had set the intention either consciously or subconsciously to be a part of this important evolutionary movement going on in the world, and to bring my best talents and passions to the fore so I could make a positive contribution towards this movement. I could even say that my entire life has been guided by a loving, gentle hand that led me to my bus revelation—the family I was born into, the way I was raised, the loving parents I had. Our formative childhood years are incredibly important as they inform everything else that happens in our later adult lives. Perhaps I love to work with children so much because I was fortunate to have parents who were good, kind and patient, who did and said many things that nurtured my self-esteem.

It's the little things I remember most, like when I was leaving the house for my very first job interview after college. I can still see my mother, standing with the screen door ajar, smiling and waving as I backed the car down the driveway.

"Good luck, dear!" she said as I drove away. "You're beautiful! You're brilliant!"

I got the job.

10.

God Gives Second Chances

Things happen in their own time. Sometimes the world isn't ready for what we have to say. Sometimes *we* are not ready. Sometimes doing our best doesn't seem good enough. If we look beneath the surface, though, maybe those best efforts remain undiminished, waiting to spring forth when conditions are optimal. Maybe our acquired knowledge needs to lie in wait for other aspects of our lives to catch up. Maybe supposed failures are tremendous blessings. I was slowly coming into a new definition of failure and, more importantly, a new definition of success. More than anything, I wanted to fully be who I am, and I wanted my work to creatively reflect that.

The time was now right. The world was ready. I was ready. And the support I needed to launch my dream had finally arrived. Deepak was most gracious as he greeted me in his private office to discuss how he could offer support for the children's programming that I was readying to launch at the Chopra Center. In no time, he made a call to the director of La Costa to inquire about a space. He connected me with staff members who could help me pull it all together and even made a few personal calls to potential funders with access to large corporations. The short-term plan was to test the concept as a "children's festival" to be held during the adult retreats. If the program was well received, we would create a permanent space on the grounds of the resort.

Double Dare You

In the summer of 2003, my second shot became reality. My venture was formally launched at the Chopra Center as CosmiKids, a colorful world in which children were free to think, dream, create and explore while gradually coming to understand the special way in which they influence—and are impacted by—the world around them. Our web presence launched simultaneously. I was lucky enough to have CosmiKids on the Chopra website as their featured children's program, a counterpart to the ongoing adult workshops. If I could bring this aspect of "consciousness" down to a kid's level, it would change everything, I believed. It would change the world! I was so excited, nervous and confident during our launch—excited because I was able to pull it off in the timeframe required, nervous because I was now running on empty having funneled most of my meager income into this project for the past six months, and confident that I was on my right path—doing something I loved that would make a positive impact on today's children.

The initial CosmiKids programming was, at its core, a composite of my earlier Kids at Heart model with a metaphysical twist, and the Sri Aurobindo educative model as an underpinning. I had contemplated everything I'd experienced and studied about holistic, integrative living, and infused it with the latest and greatest futurist insights from world-respected philosophers. I had also spent months researching the field of modern-day transformative activities for children. In the process, I'd discovered many grassroots and community-based programs and activities that were sprouting up for children; many of which were being developed by parents and teachers to augment the current schooling model of strictly academics—which was becoming increasingly outdated and ineffective by the second. In my research, I could clearly see that the momentum for a bold new way to authentically educate the whole child was gaining momentum across the nation and beyond. Certainly parents—and even educators—seemed to be in distress because the old methods (even the tried and true) were no longer working for today's youth. The time was ripe for something different, a radical new way of doing things. Finally, it seemed that everything I had worked toward, beginning with Kids at Heart in the 1980s, was coming to fruition. The moment was upon me . . . upon us, as a collective society of parents, educators and people who care deeply about the younger generation and generations to come.

I certainly wasn't the first person to come up with the idea of open-minded learning beyond academics, but it was evident that the time had now come for someone to shepherd all of these marvelous people with worthwhile concepts for children into a useable, workable program. I came across many people who had great tried-and-true ideas to empower children but didn't possess the funds, business know-how, marketing experience or—most importantly—the desire to take it to the masses. I envisioned a way to pull it all together in a unique, sustainable fashion, and immediately set about gathering an eclectic mix of people together to contribute their ideas and methods to our early curriculum.

There was Alessandra Colfi, a beautiful Italian-born artist, art and play therapist who had developed a Healing Arts Play Shop that nurtured a child's creative gifts through emotional healing. Tom Kelly, a former monk, and his beautiful wife, Trish, a former showgirl, had developed a cool film-making workshop that allowed each child to showcase their special gifts. Longtime supporter, Todd Corbin, created incredible curriculum sessions, some of which were based on the seminal work of Neale Donald Walsch, author of the best-selling *Conversations with God* book series who has subsequently become an ardent supporter of CosmiKids.

Once word got out, I was contacted by the daughter of an old friend of mine. She had created hula hoops with healing herbs and crystals inside so children could twirl and whirl with a whole new twist on self-care and wanted to come to our opening, demonstrate her hoop sensation with the children and sell me some of her one-of-a-kind products. So I thought, what the heck, let's try out her nifty hoops even though I wasn't quite sure they fit into the mix. Besides, she seemed like a pretty keen person, and I'm always willing to give someone a chance to shine, if at all possible. Well, so much for giving her the benefit of the doubt! She later absconded with all of the crystal-infused hula hoops that I purchased from her. I coined it the mysterious hoop caper. I couldn't figure out what possessed her to steal them from us. I think she was expecting to meet Deepak and be on stage with him at his seminar. (This was my first experience in observing how people "change" around those they view as "celebrities.") It was amazing to me how people could misunderstand my communication to them—in this instance, for her to misinterpret attending the opening of CosmiKids as her entrée to the Chopra world and his good name. Needless to say, that was one of many instances that have helped me to develop clearer, more definitive conversations, always paraphrasing back to people my understanding of our agreement. I imagined her stealing away in the dark of the night with 10 hula hoops around her neck because she'd been cheated out of her chance to meet a famous person. We never did recover those hot hoops.

I also lined up several women who traveled from New York to offer yoga for children and two tennis pros who had invented a unique balance and coordination training tool that worked both sides of the brain. Chopra Center employee, Teresa Long, developed and taught healthy cooking classes to children based on her in-depth knowledge of ayurveda. A jewelry designer gal pal taught beading and then, with my guidance, developed her craft to include a purpose, showing children how to infuse beads with positive affirmations then wear them to ignite pint-sized super powers of the highest order. And then there was the Scrumption Machine… a bit of nostalgia from our Kids at Heart days that had survived to see another day. I had salvaged that operable, antique vending machine from the basement of an abandoned house on the lot next to my family's company building. What a find! It held great sentimental value for me. I had used that same Scrumption Machine on the set of the MeToo children's television show pilot way back then. I still envision our Scrumption Machine in the lunchrooms of schools across the country, filled with healthy Willy-Wonka-themed snacks like Yibbly Bits, Liscious Snips, Tummy Yums, Chopra Granola and Koo-Koo Nuts, fruit strips, mango chips, and yogurt-covered raisins and organic pretzels filled with peanut butter.

> *Crafting and creating personal items and infusing them with positive affirmations works just as well for adults, too.*

We launched at the end of June, just in time for the center's popular weeklong *Seduction of the Spirit* seminar. I held a media night prior to the launch for neighbors in the community, friends, children, the media, curriculum collaborators and the La Costa and Chopra staff. It was a huge success. Most importantly, the children and parents seemed to love it. The *LA Times* covered the event. Their senior journalist, whose name was something cool like Sunny Moon, totally got CosmiKids and wrote about it beautifully. The *LA Times* photographer who accompanied her came over to me afterwards and said, "Thank you for having us out today. All morning, I was covering a car crash with photos of the accident, people in grief and scenes of destruction and despair. This is really a breath of fresh air. I feel so uplifted and good in here." The *LA Times* feature led to write-ups in *The London Times* and *Tokyo Times*. And *The Wall Street Journal* included CosmiKids in an article they published about unique summer camp experiences for kids.

But for me, the best part of this whole endeavor was observing the reactions of children and parents as they participated in these festivals. I noticed that oftentimes when someone would enter the CosmiKids theatre, as we now call it, something miraculous would happen. One little boy cried tears of gratitude as he told us of finding a place like CosmiKids where he felt accepted and liked by everyone. A mom opened up about her divorce during a "Course I Can" session, in which kids (and adults) are encouraged to blow their emotions into balloons, decorate them and watch as they float away. The father of an autistic boy remarked that he'd not seen his son so at home in any other public environment.

Blowing sad, bad, mad feelings into a balloon is a fun, effective way to disperse any negative energy that may be impacting your mood.

Be Mindful of What You Wish For

I was on a high. As the weeks went by, more and more parents who visited the Chopra Center expressed interest in our program. Word slowly spread up and down the coast of California and beyond. Suddenly, people from all over the world began writing, wanting to know how they could have a CosmiKids in their home town. I had always considered La Costa to be a testing ground and, once I had a successful working prototype there, had planned on expanding and duplicating it elsewhere. It was from this multitude of email requests that I first began to seriously explore the idea of a franchise model. I still needed a plan, some people power and money to fuel it. But from this feedback, at least I knew I was onto something that today's parents truly wanted.

Though well received by parents, in the eyes of Chopra Center management, CosmiKids seemed to remain something simply to send the kids off to while the parents attended Chopra events. After all, they were in the business of empowering adults. Though wonderful in their dealings with me, it soon became obvious that the management didn't have the time or interest in pursuing CosmiKids as a permanent offering.

The fact that CosmiKids festivals were held only intermittently at La Costa was creating a big drain on my personal reserves with little opportunity to reverse the flow. I managed to make it through those lean months, but I knew I had to find a way to increase revenues, retool the sessions to make them more cost-efficient and create more income for myself. I knew the writing was on the wall when I learned that owing to their own concerns of scheduling space with their landlord at the La Costa Resort and Spa, the Chopra Center was increasingly having to hold their seminars off site at other resorts in San Diego. Without a permanent space to hold the festivals, I would have to look elsewhere. While leaving the security of the Chopra Center behind me and branching out on my own was an unnerving prospect, I was excited to do so, knowing that I could comfortably dwell in a state of trust about the future. I will always remain grateful that they gave me a chance. It was all I ever wanted.

For the following few months or so, I worked on developing a model for the CosmiKids experience that would reflect the core concepts and original charm of the Chopra Camp sessions and also be portable, duplicable, trainable and cost efficient. I began to build a small team to help with research and development, training and marketing. I already had a dozen or so loyal, hard-working volunteers.

I kept my intentions and faith strong and watched for the little miracles that happened regularly. As investment monies dribbled in from friends, neighbors and supporters across the country to keep me temporarily afloat, I began to refine the stations in terms of usability, developmental appropriateness and visual appeal. Week by week, things seemed to miraculously happen to keep me going financially. One day, for example, two of my neighbors, with whom I'd shared many fun dinners, approached me about investing in my concept. They had both made it big in computer software sales years prior and were currently dabbling in real estate development. I was touched that they believed in me, my abilities and the creative vision that I held.

Open Minds, Pure Potential
By the time I created CosmiKids, I already knew that I wanted certain "higher consciousness" principles to be the underpinning of it. Of course, there's no denying that academics, athletics and extracurricular activities are central components of a child's upbringing. I've always believed that with the added dimension of self-exploration, children can develop the necessary sense of sense of self-worth and confidence to achieve their full potential. Rather than focusing on external rewards, I wanted to create an environment that encouraged children to explore who they truly are in mind, body and spirit—their likes and dislikes, their greatest joys and

deepest fears, and how they relate to the world and the people in it. I wanted to help them learn to trust their intuition and how to tell the difference between what is authentic and what is unnecessary noise. I envisioned that with each new revelation a child would have in this nurturing environment, this amusement park for the spirit, his or her sense of confidence would be strengthened, forming a solid foundation of self-esteem that would exist no matter the situation because it's pure, true and organic, not fashioned by peer pressure or socially imposed guidelines.

So I based the CosmiKids curriculum on universal concepts and principles that I wanted to see augmented in the world: passion, trust, courage, freedom, intuition, compassion, gratitude, confidence, wisdom and inspiration. With these guiding principles, I expanded and enhanced our now trademarked Stations of Discovery: interactive activities that are intentionally designed to engage and empower kids to boundlessly create and express themselves while fostering a sense of independence and self-mastery. Of course, the kids aren't aware that this is what they are doing. All they know is that they are having fun.

As CosmiKids was growing up, I wanted to build a work atmosphere for employees, volunteers, vendors and the public that mirrored the kind of space we were creating for children. The best way I knew to do that was for me to speak, act, embody and intend for it to be so. It's *Proclaiming your intent sets energy into motion.*

funny, but over and over again I've found that when we proclaim an honest intent to become a better person in some way, all sorts of amazing things start to happen that spawn inner growth and offer key opportunities for deeper insight into the self. As I was to learn (and had experienced already), this growth is not always comfortable, but if we can find meaning in the discomfort and view it as a sign of gaining wisdom, these occurrences can take on a whole new dimension. Personal issues are magically brought to the surface to be acknowledged and transmuted into something that works *for* us as opposed to against us.

For me, creating a space for children to fully be who they are slowly began to bring up my own issues and potential blockages related to living authentically and freely speaking my truth. Time and time again, whenever something was bothering me, I would be faced with the decision to either speak or hold my peace. When I chose silence, as I had so many times in my childhood, it became awkward, painful and completely nonproductive. As I gained courage over the years to speak up, I was met in most cases with the other person's truth, as well. Again, this is a good thing…but not always comfortable or easy to deal with. I found that some people who chose to work at CosmiKids early on couldn't handle the freedom they were given to be fully who they are, and, at times, I didn't know how to smooth them through this, either—so I take responsibility for that. In other instances, people took advantage of my good nature by not taking responsibility for their actions or leaving important tasks undone; I've learned to address red flags as soon as they crop up. Through it all, one thing was clear to me: in order for CosmiKids to sustain itself and remain a light-filled haven for children, I, as its genesis point, needed to "keep my own yard clean" and continually do my own personal work. I discovered that those who could be open and authentic in return thrived in our company environment. To this day, I put my attention on clear communication. It's an ongoing process. I still forget occasionally, but the times of not remembering are becoming less and less.

And so it became apparent that if this mission (as I was increasingly coming to see it) was to become what my heart and soul revealed to me, then I would have to embody the principles it stood for. I had to live them daily. I mean really live them, 24/7. Trust, compassion, courage, and truth became my watch words. I knew how my life had shifted simply from adopting a committed posture of gratitude. When I began to be thankful for even the seemingly difficult times, they became less painful and far more insightful. Increased blessings and subtle states of grace were sent my way. I'd be standing on a street corner or sitting in a meeting and, at once, be overcome by a glimpse of the future so startlingly real that my eyes would well up with tears. I would see CosmiKids in its entirety, impacting the world and lighting up a sure path for nurturing today's youth. This would come in instantaneous flashes.

As CosmiKids slowly matured, my perspective widened and became a lens through which I witnessed daily acts of wonder that I'm quite sure I had missed before. I became more watchful, more attentive to the daily dance of miracles. Many blessings came through the children in my midst. Other blessings came by watching gruff, even mean-spirited people become patient, lighter and more loving after spending time in our play space. Throughout it all, I kept working at being fully me: a spiritual warrior for 21st Century youth in consignment-store kitsch and second-hand Prada shoes.

PLERKing in the New Paradigm

The term "new business paradigm," or NBP, has been a buzz-phrase in the New Thought community for some time. Authors such as Michael Ray, Gary Zukav, Marilyn Ferguson, Fred Kofman and Peter Senge have given voice to this new way of doing business in the 21ˢᵗ Century. While it means many things to many people, my definition of the NBP continues to be shaped by my living it—moment by moment and one day at a time.

I wanted to create a business based on gratitude not greed, trust not fear, allowing not forcing, knowing not just know-how, collaboration not competition, higher guidance not deeper pockets, attraction not just promotion, process not end-product, and the whimsy of play not the drudgery of labor—or, better yet, the seamless integration of PLERK: play and work. For me, it's not just a work style; it's a way of being 24/7. I simply wanted to sculpt my own designer-culture of business that reflected who I am on my spiritual path.

When I look back on what hasn't worked in developing CosmiKids, more often than not I find it's something that caused me to veer from my desired path of authentic business practices. When we are rushed, making decisions out of fear or straying from our inner knowing, the result is most often not in our best interest—or anyone else's, for that matter. This can only be resolved minute by minute through choosing love not fear. But in retrospect, hasn't it all worked?

Don't be rushed into making decisions, and don't act out of fear. Remember, all the answers we need are inside us. So take time to check in with your intuition. If you listen to your inner guidance you won't make a wrong decision.

11.

We Already Have Everything We Need

The universe brings forth everything we need . . . and everyone. During those formative months, I was fortunate to meet many people who turned up to act as curriculum developers, investors, neighborhood supporters, life teachers and business consultants, all nurturing CosmiKids through its stages of puberty. To this day, I do my best to honor each one on our website and through my public and written testimonials to their good works and pure hearts—starting with our very first investor and supporter, Todd Corbin. He believed in me and CosmiKids even before it launched at the Chopra Center.

Little did I know when sitting at my favorite hair salon in Pittsburgh, readying myself for my night on the town with friends, that just a week prior, I had been sitting right next to Todd and his wife at a seminar some 3,000 miles away. My cell phone rang and I answered it, glancing at my halfway-cut hair in the mirror.

"Hi, Judy!" It was Leanne Backer, head educator and friend from the Chopra Center. "Didn't you just attend the Debbie Ford seminar that we held here last weekend?" She asked.

"Yes." I said, recalling Debbie's memorable weekend on building relationships and embracing our shadow side.

"There was a married couple from Cleveland who also attended." Leanne continued. "The young man's name was Todd. He came up to me after the morning session and wanted to know more about the children's program we're launching in June. He was very excited and wanted to know how he could find out more. He just called me again. He arrived home this morning and I wanted to check with you first before giving him your number."

"Why, sure, Leanne, thanks for asking. I'm tickled that he's interested!"

"Where are you?" she asked.

"I'm just a few hours from Cleveland." This coincidence piqued my curiosity.

"Isn't that trippy!" Leanne laughed. "Six days ago you were both in the same room in California without knowing each other, and now you're both in another part of the country and about to connect."

Todd called me within minutes of hanging up with Leanne. He told me that he and his wife, Stacy, had been sitting directly in front of me that whole weekend. Todd wanted to learn more about CosmiKids and agreed to drive to Pennsylvania. With my newly coifed hairdo and business plan in hand, we met for lunch the following day. By the end of our meal, Todd had pledged $5,000 along with his support to help in any way possible. At that moment, I felt as if a big emotional hurdle had been overcome. I had my first investor! Someone besides me believed enough in the concept to pledge their money in support of it! I was thrilled. I remember being with Jennifer shortly after that meeting. "Just you watch, Judy, she said, "this is just the beginning." Something within me rang true.

There were many such serendipitous meetings and alliances soon to form. I had been in telephone contact with a homeopath in Ireland who had developed a line of children's essences with her young nephews. I wanted to explore incorporating their healing tonics into our curriculum as tools that children could use to balance themselves or improve their moods. Indigo Essences, as they were called, are mineral essences that are like a first aid kit for feelings. "Good vibes in a bottle," as their website touts, that can help ward off bullies, soften bad dreams, diffuse anger, or build courage. In my conversations with Ann she had told me that she came up with the idea for essences after years of listening to children telling her about things that bother them. She mentioned a new magazine that was about to be launched that I should check into. Ann felt the magazine, which was called *Children of the New Earth,* and had been started by a British woman who was living in San Diego, would quickly become a valuable resource guide for modern, conscious parents. Ann recommended I immediately get in touch with "this fiery Brit" with the strawberry blonde hair, thus paving the way for my meeting with Sandie Sedgbeer, who soon became our second investor, my dear, dear friend and trusted collaborator. Through Sandie, I met Gail Torr, another spitfire Brit who has become our phenomenal publicist.

One day, I decided to portray graphically on a wall mural all of the connections, networks and clusters of amazing people I'd met through CosmiKids. On big sheets of paper with multicolored markers, I mind-mapped how this-person-led-me-to-that-person-who-led-me-to-meet-the-next-person. I put each name in a brightly colored bubble, beginning with Leanne. Before long, one whole wall was practically covered with sheets of brightly colored names. I continued this mural for weeks, adding people whom I'd forgotten, or new acquaintances that seemed to pop up almost daily. I think this "visual Rolodex" is a great tool for budding entrepreneurs. It solidified for me that there really is a grander plan at work beyond our work-a-day world, which then deepened and expanded my sense of gratitude at the magnificence and intricacies of the divine orchestrating powers around us. The mural reminds me that if I have a desire to meet someone or get anything accomplished, I only have to look up at that graphic presentation of what's possible and set the intent. From that, someone will come along or something will happen to connect the dots and bring my wish to speedy fruition.

Creating a visual Rolodex is a great way of discovering how we are all connected, and how synchronicity plays a valuable role in your life.

Here's a few short examples of how this manifested in my life.

The Flying Water Glass

On the verge of leaving the Chopra Center and going on my own, I wanted to collaborate with others who could help me expand my vision. Where would I find these future colleagues? And how would I compensate them? With trust and self-assurance, I forged ahead with multi-pronged action steps to take CosmiKids to the next level, all the while believing that the people and resources the company needed in order to realize its fullest potential would present themselves. My long list of action steps began each day with a simple ritual. I'd wake up with a warm feeling of appreciation for everything I had at the present moment. It may sound trite, but I believe that a posture of gratitude is what sets the tone for attracting all good things for CosmiKids and into my life in general. All of my business decisions throughout the day stem from that early morning precedent.

At this time, I was most in need of a curriculum director, someone to run the CosmiKids festivals. I wanted to be freed up to expand and grow the business and I wanted a spiritually-aligned someone to work with who would train people, run the sessions and help develop new programs. It was just before Thanksgiving. How appropriate! Sandie had been suggesting for some time that I meet a woman named Lena. We'd heard from several respected sources that Lena was doing interesting and transformative work with children, teens and parents in the form of camps, counseling sessions, workshops and festivals. Her name kept popping up on the cosmic radar screen. When that kind of thing happens, I pay attention.

It had become increasingly apparent to me that I no longer wanted to coordinate and implement all of the CosmiKids festivals myself. My heart was in building a global business that matched the huge vision I had tucked in my heart sleeve. I also wanted to augment the CosmiKids experience with more stations, more adventure and more innovative content. Sandie felt that Lena had the right heart space—hard working, loving, and with a legion of volunteers and great ideas. We met at a casual restaurant called Mimi's.

I knew the moment I laid eyes on Lena (and my telepathic sensors on her energy field) that she was a magnificent being. She had beautiful eyes, a loving, open smile, and laughed so easily and often. She came armed with a photo album of her children's activity camps, some articles she'd written and lots of stories about her hopes and dreams. Within 30 minutes of meeting Lena, out of my lips came a statement that surprised even me.

"I believe you are going to run CosmiKids!"

Was I really saying this about my "baby," that I had been so careful to nurture each step of the way so far . . . to a total stranger!

Just then, a glass of water flew across the room, seemingly out of nowhere, and fell to the floor near our table. Where did it come from? Who knows?! Stunned, and somewhat damp, we looked at each other for a few seconds then laughed; as we knew some mighty energy had just blessed our meeting. Shortly thereafter, Lena came on board and immediately donned many hats: training and session director, curriculum developer, creative manager, marketing advisor and Mother Teresa to all of the employees, children, parents and vendors. Finding Lena was nothing short of a godsend. I was then able to put my sights on empowering others, vision-holding, co-creating and networking like crazy.

When things got kicking with Lena and we really needed someone to spearhead the sales effort, Mark, a veteran salesperson and spiritual warrior, turned up through a synchronistic turn of events at a program CosmiKids had offered high in the mountains of North Carolina. Mark quickly relocated from Texas to join us and became a key, valued player. God bless Mark. He uncomplainingly undertook whatever was needed in those early days to get the job done—everything from hanging curtains and leading our intention-setting workshops to smoothing the ruffled feathers of sensitive co-workers and standing by me in times of turmoil and sudden change.

When we needed an IT whiz, one showed up with a smile and a commitment to support our technology needs. When we needed a cosmic wall muralist and help with curriculum development, Uran surfaced to fulfill both those needs and more; A loving navigator for peace who remains with us today and shines brightly in many important areas of our evolving company. Cabinet builder? We got it. Not by looking in the phone book but by intending and allowing. A light and color therapist? No prob. When we need a seasoned operations director? Yep, along came Lori, bearing a baby Buddha on her hip to boot! Her toddler, Jack William, is a loveable and powerful little being who displayed many psychic talents early on that amazed us all. Like the day he favored a toy so much that it literally followed him and his mom, fueled by nothing other than its own wheel power. No wind, no incline and no human pushed it along. It was clearly Jack's focused desire. Lori later told me that odd things like this happen all the time around her little Buddha boy.

Each and every one came, not always in the package we imagined or the timeframe we might have hoped for. But they all came—and still continue to come—without fail.

Two Hip

Over the years, I've learned that "already having everything we need" can sometimes come in the form of discomfort, pain and, yes, more opportunities for personal growth. We not only have within us the answers but the questions, the homework, the tests, the tutors and the scholarship dollars, just waiting to be awarded. In 2004, I didn't have to look any farther than my own body to find a great teacher with all the answers.

Even though I lived within a hop, skip and jump from a gym in 2004, I wasn't doing much hopping and skipping back then. And I definitely wasn't jumping. Okay, let's say I was doing my own style of Hip Hop. The pain in my right hip had gradually worsened each day. Walking became sheer torture. With every step a struggle, just getting where I needed to go became a chore. Two years prior, I'd had my left hip replaced with a titanium and ceramic fixture. The recovery was gruesome for the first two weeks but soon after my hip was pain-free. At the time, my right hip hadn't been a problem. With my new hardware installed, I had been once again able to work out at the gym and walk comfortably for miles.

Still relatively young and with an active lifestyle, I was amazed to have been diagnosed with osteoarthritis. Apparently, my mother's health had been compromised while she was pregnant with me. This had resulted in my developing a condition of hip dysplasia, which brought about early onset arthritis. I had only ever heard about canine hip dysplasia, a common cause of limping in dogs. Well, there I was, limping with the canines and wanting to find a way to feel better fast.

Always willing to explore my emotional depths, I was determined to get to the root of any problem that may have contributed to my health condition. Obviously, I believe that our physical well being has a direct link to our personal growth lessons, which are, in turn, affected by the degree of balance and harmony within our emotional bodies. In addition to hips being associated with our ability to move forward in life, this body part is also associated with one's outlook on abundance, ability to receive, and the capacity to stand on one's own two feet as an independent, capable being. Well-known author Louise Hay, who sat next to me in yoga class on many occasions, wrote the best seller *You Can Heal Yourself,* which became my bedside companion during those painful months. I had read all about alternative mind-body healing techniques, and since I didn't want to go through the pain of surgery and recovery twice, I decided to explore the natural self-healing landscape.

I first made a major diet overhaul, cutting out all dairy, meat and processed foods (which I ate in small quantities, anyway). I then began intensive one-on-one Iyengar yoga sessions twice weekly to open my hip joints and increase flexibility. When none of that seemed to help, I scheduled a five-day pancha karma detox retreat in Albuquerque, New Mexico at an ayurveda-based healing center led by Dr. Vasant Lad. Ayurveda (a Sanskrit word that means "the science of life") is considered by many scholars to be the oldest healing science. While all of the alternative healing methods served me well and cleansed my system, I was still in pain. Gradually I came to the realization that medical surgery is God's work, too. It seems that I had gone to great lengths in search of a cure when all along I had the best answer right under my nose. I even had a referral to a reputable orthopedic surgeon to do the surgery. And he was located in my native hometown where I could be surrounded by family and loved ones during my recuperation. I was just frightened of going through those hellacious 14 days after surgery.

I also questioned in my quiet hours why I wasn't able to heal it myself. It's like the story of the man in a flood, praying to God for help. He was sent a boat, a plane and other support, turning them all down, saying he was waiting for a sign from God, when all along, God was speaking to him. It simply came in packages he wasn't open to receiving. Once I accepted that surgery was an answer to my prayers, I scheduled to have the second hip surgically replaced.

This second time around, I took a more holistic, proactive stance with my recovery period. I employed a method that I found online called *Prepare for Surgery, Heal Faster.* It contained a book and audio program that helped me immensely. The easy-to-follow program began a month before my surgery date with suggestive tapes and relaxation methods for quieting the mind and soothing my nervous system. Since I'd been a long-time meditator this was easy for me. The kit also included five affirmative statements to be given to my anesthesiologist and surgeon to read aloud as I was going under anesthesia. *Judy's body heals quickly... Judy's surgery is a success... Judy's recovery is miraculous and pain-free ...* They agreed to do this.

As a result, I experienced very little pain during my recuperation. I was up and walking without the aid of painkillers the day after surgery. My overall recovery was speedier, which gave me more time to focus on my personal growth as it related to hip issues. I went deep inside and explored my willingness to receive all good things in life, my sense of deservedness with respect to financial abundance, and my burning desire to speak my truth. It became clear during those times of quiet reflection that I was maturing as a spiritual being who was having an adventure-filled human experience. I also used the downtime to draft a business plan, design décor for an expanded CosmiKids play space, and begin to map out its architectural design with a dear friend, who became our founding architect. I saw no reason to waste time with medication. I renewed my system the natural way . . . with inspired work!

Now it was time to segue into my next period of discovery—one that would include a pivotal meeting, a quirky brainstorm and the chance of a lifetime.

12.

Boldness Really Does Have Genius, Power and Magic in It

I've always been drawn to the life and times of pioneers like Albert Einstein, Walt Disney, Stephen Jobs, Madonna and the CEO's of various innovative start-ups. They have all displayed an element of unconventionality that intrigues me. When I read about people like that, it inspires me to be my bold self, regardless of what others may think. Sometimes, being a little daring provides entrée into opportunities that I wouldn't have been given otherwise. In this chapter, I will share a few stories that demonstrate just that—including how I ended up working with one of the nation's top franchising organizations (and how events conspired to lead me to them).

> **What you can do, or dream you can do, begin it!**
> **Boldness has genius, power and magic in it.**
>
> —*Johann Wolfgang Goethe*

Encouraged by these words, spoken centuries ago, I set the intention to find a way to duplicate the CosmiKids experience in many locations. I knew that I would need to formalize all of this with a top-notch business plan. Given my short-lived experience with the restaurants, the idea of franchising was in the back of my mind. However—and this is a huge however—I had somewhat limited experience writing business plans and duplicating a retail concept, and very limited knowledge about franchising. I wanted to align with the best of the best in this regard but I didn't know anyone and, besides, had no funds to pay a top-shelf franchise consultant. I didn't even have a budget to get assistance on the business plan.

Some time earlier while creating my mural of connections, I had met with another entrepreneur at a wonderful local hangout (housed in an old train station along the Pacific Coast Highway) to talk about incorporating his product and activity set into our offerings at CosmiKids. I had been looking for something to add a bit of cardio work and balance training for children, and Jack's product seemed to be the ticket. Unbeknownst to me, Jack had invited one of his key investors to the meeting, a man named Arthur Lipper, who just happened to be the former publisher of *Venture Magazine*. Arthur immediately took a liking to the CosmiKids concept.

"If you ever decide to franchise your concept, call this guy," he said, scribbling a number on a scrap of paper. "He's the best in the business."
I thanked him and stuffed it in my pocket. That evening, I had added an Arthur Lipper circle to my bubble wall. As calls and emails of inquiry about CosmiKids escalated on the Chopra Center web site. I reached for the paper scrap. I would soon add the name Don Boroian to my mural, surrounded by a bright red circle.

Something Ventured, Everything Gained
"Central Casting could not have come up with a more perfect character to run CosmiKids than you, Judy," declared this same Don Boroian.

I took this comment as an extreme compliment, especially coming from the chairman of one of the country's largest and most successful franchise companies. This remark was an about face from Don's original assessment of me as a business woman. When I first met with him to discuss building CosmiKids into an international franchise operation, he had asked who was going to run the company for me.

"I am," I said. God had given me a second chance and I knew I would have everything I needed to be an effective CEO.

"What?" He laughed out loud. "You don't have the background for it." Here we go, again, I thought: *who do you think you are?*

"I don't care," I responded, nonchalantly. "One of THE most important things to me is to birth and ground this business along the lines that I envision."

It took a while to prove to Don that I was the exact right person—which is why his Central Casting comment was so luscious. Even more luscious, however, was the way in which I had managed to get Don to meet with me in the first place.

A few weeks earlier, I had dug out the scrap of paper that Arthur Lipper had given me that day in Encinitas. On it was the number for Francorp, the franchise consulting company founded by Don in 1976, which now handles 40 percent of all franchising in the US and serves 45 countries.

I did some research online and found that Francorp was the only such firm to offer clients a one-stop service by coordinating strategic planning, legal, operations and marketing services under one roof. There list of clients was impressive – McDonald's, Blockbuster Video, Ace Hardware, ARCO AM/PM Mini Markets, Hershey Foods, Ryder Trucks, Popeye's Fried Chicken, Nutrasweet, Nestle, John Deere, Texaco, and Valvoline, to name a few. I was excited. Francorp was exactly what I needed and wanted!

Eagerly, I read on. "Francorp receives more than 10,000 inquiries every year from companies who want to franchise," their website stated. "Our analysts screen them down to 800 companies, and we then accept 100 projects a year for development."

As I did the math, my hopes began to dwindle. The odds of meeting Francorp's strict criteria were exactly 99 to one against me! I closed down my laptop.

Hmmm, I pondered. *This might be a lot harder than I thought.*

Then … *So what?* Another part of me countered. *Nothing ventured, nothing gained.*

Fortune favors the brave, they say… so don't be fainthearted. You'll be amazed at what can happen when you dare to live audaciously!

In a spirit of dogged determination, I fired up my laptop once more, punched in Francorp's URL and immediately took their onscreen survey to determine if my concept was franchiseable. CosmiKids passed the test.

Spurred on by this positive feedback, I picked up the phone and dialed the number on the scrap of paper.

Ring…ring.

I formulated in my mind the voice mail message that I intended to leave.

Ring…ring.

"Hello, this is Don Boroian."

What? I froze in shock. *An actual person on the other end?* I don't know who I had expected to reach—a company operator, an administrative assistant, someone's voice mail—but certainly not the founder and CEO of the company.

Recovering my poise, I quickly explained to Don how I had gotten his number from Arthur Lipper, that I'd been on his website, taken Francorp's pretest and now wished to meet with him to discuss franchising the next big thing in children's educational enrichment.

Don listened patiently, and then politely invited me to attend a Francorp franchise seminar he was going to be conducting in Los Angeles the following week.

I was ecstatic. The ease with which it had all happened was yet one more piece of evidence for me that I must be on the right path, because the universe was working hand in hand with me.

The following Saturday found me up with the lark—like a kid who couldn't wait for the rest of the household to wake and start celebrating her birthday. Somewhere inside me, I had the strongest sense that something magical was going to happen that day.

At the hotel, I found a seat in the front row of the audience and settled down to wait for Don Boroian's appearance. From the moment he walked into the room, I immediately liked his demeanor.

"Okay, all of you are business people," he said in greeting. "I want you to keep your cell phones on and answer them if they ring."

Huh? I thought. *That's an interesting twist on things. Most speakers immediately insist that everyone check their cell phones are turned off. This is going to be interesting.*

Twice during his presentation, Don answered his phone, and politely and patiently provided his callers with the information they needed. And then immediately continued where he had left off speaking to the audience without missing a beat.

Wow! If that's the kind of 24/7 focus and accessibility he offers his clients, I thought, *I want to work with him.*

I spent the entire morning, glued to my seat, taking in every word that fell from Don's lips. It didn't matter that I was unfamiliar with half the terms Don was throwing around—this man was talking my language!

Every attendee had been offered five minutes to speak with Don personally at the end of the seminar. I had purposely prescheduled the last meeting time slot of the day because I had wanted him to leave with CosmiKids on his mind. As I made a beeline for the podium, I felt as if destiny was knocking and I couldn't have been more happy, hopeful and excited to open the door and see what the world of franchising had to offer. It felt like I'd found a missing piece in developing the next stage of my concept. The conviction behind Don's words seemed like the perfect match for me and CosmiKids.

Both nervous and excited, I was, admittedly, a little outrageous during that initial meeting. I remember standing in front of the room—my hair in spiky pigtails and a huge, blooming hibiscus pinned to my lapel,—playfully banging on the table between us, declaring: WE'VE ALREADY GOT INTEREST FROM PEOPLE IN 12 COUNTRIES. WE'RE GOING TO CHANGE THE WORLD WITH THIS NEW LIFESTYLE FRANCHISE!

Don's faced remained impassive. Finally, when I had finished my impassioned presentation, he looked me squarely in the eye, and with zero emotion said:

"Your business plan is not atypical of what we see with a lot of wide-eyed entrepreneurs who have a great idea and are trying to articulate it in a plan; it's 99 percent about the technology [the concept] and only one percent addressing business issues."

With an air of finality he closed up my business plan and handed it back to me. "It's a wonderfully articulated dialogue of what you do but it doesn't address corporate formation and general admin costs, national marketing, staffing needs, governmental and legal compliances, accounting issues, construction, and so on. In short, it's got more holes than a piece of Swiss cheese."

My face fell.

With his poker face intact, Don went on: "You're not ready for prime time, Judy. We typically don't take on a project unless it's already a successful program. We basically clone successful businesses so they can be replicated by others."

Not wanting this to be the end of the yellow brick road, I asked The Wizard if there was anything else I could do.

"Raise 125 grand," he said as he walked away to catch an LAX shuttle. "That's for the full package. That's what it'll cost to take CosmiKids and franchise it internationally."

Thanks to my two new wonder-hips, I was able easily to keep up with Don as he strode toward the shuttle.

"Call me when you've raised the money." he said, as he stepped aboard the bus.

Unwilling to let it all end like that, I blurted out the first thing that came to mind.

"Can we work out a payment plan? I could get a bank loan."

Don stopped, turned, looked at me, and, poker-faced to the last, re-peated: "Call me when you get the money, we'll talk then."

As the shuttle doors closed, he offered one last parting shot: "And if all else fails, buy a ski mask—those banks have surveillance cameras."

The shuttle drove off, leaving me enveloped in exhaust fumes. Should I be insulted or amused? I took my piece of Swiss cheese and went home.

On the two-hour drive back to Carlsbad, I sensed the familiar bubble of enthusiasm that typically precedes my madcap ideas beginning to well up inside me. I wasn't stressing about the *10,000-to-100 odds.* I wasn't fix-ated on where the hell I'd get $125,000. I just drove on the freeway and followed the freefall. You see, for me, the notion of unlimited potential isn't just lip service. It's the kiss of real success. I dwell in it because I believe that's where living really is. If something feels right, or fun, or aligned with what thrills me most, I proceed full-speed ahead. The outcome will take care of itself. If there's a will, there's a way. Even with Mr. Poker Face. In that moment, cruising the 101 Freeway and imaging the process was joy enough for me.

A Ski Mask from eBay

Arriving home after the Francorp seminar, I wasn't in a mood to follow convention. Determined as ever and jazzed by the car-ride, I cooked up a plan.

First, I rewrote the business plan. Next, I collected the articles about CosmiKids that had been published in *The Wall Street Journal, London Times, Tokyo Times* and *Los Angeles Times,* together with the 100-plus emails I'd received from around the world requesting CosmiKids franchise information, and anything else I could gather that offered evidence of a serious brand in the making. Finally, I logged onto eBay and searched for the *piece de resistance* item in my Big Plan. There it was: a three-holed, black-knit ski mask. Perfect!

When the mask arrived by mail a few days later, I strategically placed it atop the printed materials with a note that said:

Plan A: Francorp invests $125,000 in return for CosmiKids stock.

Plan B: Francorp invests $60,000 with a loan of $65,000 to be paid back with revenues from franchise fees.

Plan C: I enlist your help; it involves the ski mask.

Don was either going to like it or think I was nuts.

Bingo! It was the ski mask that got him! A month later I flew to Chicago for a meeting at Francorp's corporate office. I didn't tell Don beforehand that all I'd managed to scrape together was $2,000—only $123,000 short of the larger target, and $13,000 less than Francorp's initial fee!

Without preamble Don asked: "Did you raise the money?"

"I have two thousand of it," I said in all honesty.

"Well, the meetings are set so let's see what you've got." Don said, instructing everyone to enter the boardroom. He didn't appear to be miffed that I was wasting his time. Perhaps he saw a little of himself in me; after all, he too had once been a budding entrepreneur.

I'll never forget that first pitch to Francorp's team of 10 specialists. Each one was extremely well mannered, meticulously groomed, and had the same air of professional confidence and wisdom that I'd seen in Don. Then there was me, be-bopping into the room like a kid who had just been handed a free ride-all-day pass at the Magic Kingdom. The night before in my hotel room, in addition to nailing my sales pitch, I laid out two possible outfits for the presentation. *Hmm… Should I go with my corporate garage band/rap star look? Or a more understated motif: pinstripe jacket, starched oxford shirt with loosely knotted man's tie, black fishnets and white kitten heels?* (I chose the latter.) Surrounded by suits, I didn't feel like a fish out of water. I just imagined that I'd leapt into another bowl and now it was time to swim around in it. Don entered the room last, still looking stoic, but I sensed an air of kindness about him, as well. He introduced me by retelling the ski mask story.

Then the curtains parted, the band died down and I was on. For the next 30 minutes, I sang the CosmiKids theme song; how I felt this concept was important in the larger scope of humanity, and why I believed it could be a successful franchise. I referenced Howard Schultz's *Pour Your Heart into It: How Starbucks Built a Company One Cup at a Time.* "People said they were crazy, that no one in America was going to pay $3.50 for a cup of coffee. But Starbucks isn't about coffee, really. It's about capturing a 21st Century lifestyle! Community building! Relationships! Interconnectedness! Putting people before product! Corporate social responsibility!" I said. "CosmiKids would be just like that, only our 'little beans' would be in human form."

I must have done something right because the Francorp team later informed me that my concept had great potential—not just financially but for humanity. They immediately agreed to help me re-sculpt the business plan for just $10,000. *Gulp!* I didn't have that amount of money, as my alimony checks were running out.

AND I'd put every spare penny into CosmiKids.

AND I had no immediate funding prospects.

AND… "I'll get the money somehow, just wait and see." I solemnly promised Don. "And I am a quick study, so you won't have to worry about having to spoon feed me through the revisions," I further assured him.

From Chicago, I flew directly to Boston where I was scheduled to do a CosmiKids program in several child enrichment centers. The next day, I had a friendly lunch with an acquaintance. We caught up with our lives over salad and iced tea. I didn't mention anything about my financial

Focus on the positive; don't give energy to the negative.

needs. Instead I focused on everything that was positive, happily sharing all of the exciting developments surrounding CosmiKids.

Out of the blue she said: "Judy, I love what you're doing. I'd like to invest some money." Honest to goodness, that's just how it happened. During my brief stay in Boston, she conferred with her financial manager and wrote a check for $8,000. I was blown away. It was exactly the amount that I needed to pay Francorp. And I hadn't even thought about asking her to invest!

That act of generosity and shared belief in my dream showed me that unless you ask the universe for what you want, you'll never know if there's a willing participant on the other end of that request. From that day forward, I started asking anyone within earshot if they wanted to get involved in an exciting project that was going to change the world of education. At that point, I realized that I was no longer driving the dream. It had taken on a robust, sassy life of its own. It also created a huge shift within me. Instead of asking other people for funds, I started offering them an opportunity to invest in the future of our youth—a subtle difference, but an important one.

Within 48 hours of leaving Francorp's offices, I called Don to inform him that I'd raised the balance of the money. I was ecstatic. True to form, he, of course, didn't seem in the least surprised or fazed. But then, Don's used to dealing with people who have the money and I don't think he knew how close I was to reaching the end of my rope at that point—trying to keep the business alive and make an income for myself.

Numbers are My Friend

According to the bestselling book *A Course in Miracles,* "Freedom from illusions lies only in not believing in them." I decided to put this to a conscious test with something that has always given me trepidation: number crunching. The continuation of my Francorp story illustrates how I essentially overcame my long-term numbers phobia in 48 hours. (Yes, we can wipe clean longstanding "issues" when we do conscious inner work and believe in a higher power. No need for years of therapy!)

My first order of business with this organization was to provide them with a sample pro forma of what a week at CosmiKids looked like in terms of number of classes held, price points, retail items sold, operational agenda, staffing overview, costs and expected revenues. This was going to be challenging enough due to the fact that we hadn't yet been operational in a retail setting long enough to gauge any of these important business parameters. Even revenue was hazy. Up until that point, our CosmiKids festivals had been mobile. I was living hand-to-mouth in those early days, paying people when I could, trying to survive long enough to test the program, interest investors, and expand my company vision.

The morning after returning home from Chicago, I went to the gym to work out, came home, fueled my body and brain with oatmeal and fruit, showered, said a prayer—then got busy. As I sat down to work, I purposefully deepened my breathing pattern to relax and allow my inner guidance to kick into gear. In the Kids at Heart days, my dear accounting whiz, Jennifer, would say that I hated working with numbers. True, my mind gravitates to the fluid, creative side of things. That's my nature but it doesn't mean I couldn't accustom myself to thinking in linear, defined terms. I could change my focus with the belief that within me lies dormant an inner financial genius.

So, with that in my mind and heart, I said repeatedly (inwardly and out loud) during those next few days as I worked, that I loved numbers. I felt this with all the happiness in my being. I spoke it. I heard it. I thought it. I felt it. I actually *felt love* for numbers. My mantra was: numbers are my friends . . . numbers are my friends . . . numbers are my friends. If I could have found a bumper sticker that said "Number Lover", I would have affixed it to my SUV.

Use affirmations to love what you used to hate but need.

So, I started and ended that day and the next one with the attitude that I already knew whatever I needed to know. It's a far different attitude than the fear-based mindset of "I don't know where to begin, if I can do it right or do it at all." That causes our bodies to tighten, our minds to constrict and we begin to lose that ever-present connection to our all-knowing self. I turned around the pro forma in two days. The franchise company executives were amazed because they probably didn't think I could do it!

CEO Don told me after we met about that same pro forma, "Judy, fear is not in your vocabulary. We are impressed by your level of focus and commitment, and by the insightful questions you raised about our financial assumptions. You showed an ability to grasp the entire financial picture."

That comment warmed me so. Numbers and me have been buds ever since.

Refresh the Franchise
From the moment I began working with Francorp's inner executive circle, they impressed me as the very best, the 911 and 411 in franchising. As it turns out, it was only the beginning of the yellow brick road. I was Dorothy in a Land of Consultancy Oz. Finally, I had seasoned, professional support.

Having had a little experience in franchising through my trial-by-fire adventures in the fast food industry during the late '90s, I knew that there were some standard business codes and mores of the typical franchise model that, in some respects, were completely at odds with my collaborative, compassion-based philosophy. I had witnessed first-hand with Arby's the "us versus them" mentality that seemed to exist between franchisor and franchisee, and how little regard Arby's management seemed to have for their franchisees as people, relating to them solely through the numbers and lens of profitability. I never understood the underlying animosity. But nobody had listened to me back then. I was green and I was female. That was not the first time I'd been forced to acknowledge that my perspective and society's perspective don't always jive. I used to remain silent. But having found my courage, I no longer felt the need to keep quiet. I found my voice and articulated my thoughts and feelings regularly with everyone at Francorp.

Don and his head legal counsel, Jill, were the two people at Francorp who at times seemed to balk most at my questioning and wanting to reconfigure long-standing legal documents. As an arbitrator and mediator for the American Arbitration Association, Don is in great demand as an expert witness in franchise litigation, so he knows the importance of verbiage and clarity in legal matters with respect to the highly regulated franchise industry. As head of Francorp's legal department, Jill was responsible for drafting franchise agreements, franchise offering circulars and ancillary materials. With their combined background in litigation and their vast experience with the FTC, Don and Jill formed a strong alliance for keeping important documents just as they were. They saw no reason to change them, as no one had ever questioned them in the past, certainly not a newbie like me.

So perhaps it wasn't really surprising that when I casually mentioned to Jill that the franchise agreement sounded a little harsh to me, she quickly stated that those documents had been carefully drafted after many costly and time-consuming revisions to become the solid agreements that they were, successfully safeguarding the franchisor and upholding the sanctity of the franchise arrangement in good times and bad. Jill certainly knew what she was talking about, as she had studied comparative law at Victoria University of Wellington Law School in New Zealand, for God's sake! Still, my inner guidance told me I needed to do something to soften the negative tone of the agreement. After all, we were stating in that document how we planned to conduct business. With that language, I was setting the precedent for the working relationship with our franchisees. I knew there was a way to restate this legal document to make it more, well, "cosmic" and I was determined to find it.

I decided to form my own ad hoc committee and investigate the options. After some internal dialogue to explore who would best fill those important short-term positions, I called upon two friends who would fit the bill perfectly. Angela was a home-schooling mom, singer in a rock band, liberal social activist, child advocate, long-time volunteer at CosmiKids festivals and a kick-ass kinda gal. Jean-Pierre was a soft-spoken, spiritually aligned, retired attorney who attended a weekly networking breakfast club that I had joined a year prior. Together, we comprised the CosmiKids Legal Eagle Team. We met over several lunches and went through the franchise agreement line-by-line. Our thoughts flowed so smoothly and we had great fun. I believe Angela and Jean-Pierre knew they were part of something that was a kindly force for change. It felt worthwhile and somewhat exciting. I bought them lunch and they never charged me for their time. Together, we co-created revisions to the agreement that I was much more comfortable with. Our minor changes reflected my desire to set the tone at the outset of the franchisor/franchisee relationship, for a harmonious, collaborative, win-win union.

At first, Don bristled at the thought and expense of changing a legal document but later acquiesced to my wishes. It was the first time, to my knowledge, that Francorp had changed a legal document for someone so new to the franchise world. I applaud them for their openness. They rose to the occasion and raised the bar for enlightened business practices within the world of franchising. I was tickled to realize that my team and I were responsible for opening up other's people's eyes to a new, friendlier and more collaborative way of doing business and negotiating documents. Perhaps this was a sign of things to come—for CosmiKids and for the business world at large—a sign that, yes, we really are becoming more conscious, more compassionate, more enlightened in business and beyond.

13.

Are We Having Fund Yet?

With my team now in place and a solid plan in the works to bring CosmiKids-to the world, I began to feel even freer to think large. It felt like I had waited my whole life for this, to build my dream company and do it my way. Now, finally, the blank canvas was before me, and I could create anything my heart desired. Would my creation be Surrealist? Fauvist? Dada? Postmodern? Pre-Cosmic? It would be all of these and none of these. I would take everything I'd learned—from my father and the encounter with Mr. Higgins, all my prior entrepreneurial ventures, up to the present moment—and create my own work of art. Because I believe the essence of this new paradigm goes way beyond thinking outside the box—there IS no box, really. So why contain ourselves? Why not choose total freedom in our work? Are we alive? Are we breathing? There is no day like the present to live the fullest creative expression of ourselves. And there is no limit to the style or form that can take. There is only what we can imagine and make happen.

"Divine Supply" Economics

When I had struck out on my own from the Chopra Center, there was so much to accomplish. CosmiKids was growing up and, in many ways, so was I. Once I knew investment funds were potentially on their way, I started thinking about moving from La Costa where we had everything stored in a small garage to larger premises closer to Lena and our volunteers. Meantime, however, I was still making ends meet by scheduling CosmiKids camps in neighboring communities, at private homes and through the LA County Department of Parks and Recreation, in addition to taking steps to make good on my promise to Francorp (and to myself) to garner further funding for our growth. I was a bit nervous because my personals funds were now reaching critical stage. At the same time, I needed to be ultra confident that our best-guess numbers in the business plan were, in fact, a clear reflection of our proposed business model. Even though we had gathered seasoned professionals, concept developers and children's programming specialists, our financial projections were just that—*projections*. Other location-based companies like Gymboree, My Gym, Music and Me and Discovery Zone were profitable, so I knew it was entirely feasible. But we didn't yet have a permanent location to prove out all of this. The benefits that CosmiKids was offering children were far above and beyond physical fitness, music appreciation and eye-hand coordination talents that the current exercise and entertainment venues were providing. I knew that we were playing in a different ball park altogether. And we felt confident that we were answering a call from humanity for richer, more meaningful experiences for families. Surely, a profitability curve was in there waiting to be realized.

All of these growth pangs are what most business owners endure, but I was determined to take something of value from each experience *while* I was going through it. As I moved forward on each front, I used intention-setting to guide the process. I started by compiling a small binder of note cards with dates and intention categories. This trusty binder traveled everywhere I went. While waiting for meetings or in airports, I'd retrieve it from my purse or briefcase and read or revise them, as needed. I kept my intentions simple and clear, and stated each one in the present tense as if it had already happened. For example, I knew I wanted to find a highly conscious, amiable and expert accountant—a numbers whiz with spiritual resonance.

The more you focus your energy on what you want, the greater the chance it has of coming to fruition.

So I wrote: "I now enjoy a friendly working relationship with a highly effective, purpose-driven accountant who embraces metaphysical principles while being firmly grounded in solid business practices." The very next day, one of our collaborators called with a recommendation. What's interesting is that I hadn't asked her about this! Another intention I set was to find a personal assistant. Poof, one appeared for just the amount of time I needed her. A couple months after she resigned, I "upgraded" my intention to fit the skills and qualities I would need in a personal assistant during the company's next phase of grow. Along came another delightful person who was a perfect complement to my needs and sensibilities.

I don't mean to make it sound like intention setting gives you exactly what you want when you want it, without any hiccups along the way. But I do believe that we always get what we need—it may not be on our timetable, or in the way we wish to receive it, but the process always works. Any bumps in the road have only served to give me increased courage and an ability to

See the gifts, and be willing to accept them just as they are, even if they are different from what you envisioned.

put a finer point on my intentions. Again, my focus is on success in the present moment. Whenever roadblocks appear, instead of belaboring what isn't working, I adjust and put my attention on what I DO want. If we start from the premise that all intentions manifest, then we have to be open to receiving them as the gifts they are.

Like many entrepreneurs, the part of nurturing my enterprise that has given me the most challenges is funding. All great ideas take money to implement. We were in bona fide start-up mode and I could no longer ask people to volunteer their services and talents. And even though franchising is a self-capitalizing model, I needed to raise more money than I ever had in my life: a budget of $700,000 was required for the design and production of our nine interactive floor-model play stations; child development, business, PR, legal and accounting consultants; leasehold improvements, branding, marketing and web design; offices, admin salaries and executive team compensation.

At the time, I was clearly still experimenting with balancing tried-and-true methods of traditional fundraising with my more metaphysically-based, first-hand understanding of the Law of Attraction. On the one hand, I had teamed up with an international franchise company whose formula for success is based on cloning already proven businesses to be replicated by others. I happily labored over writing a full-blown standard business plan, and worked with my attorney to draft a detailed private placement memorandum to be used as our cornerstone funding document. Even in the new business paradigm, we can't throw the baby out with the bathwater. It's more effective to take what feels right from the Harvard Business School-type models and blend it into the latest and greatest spiritual laws for success. I needed to learn everything I learned in order to effectively run the business. A multitude of entrepreneurs before me have "gone the traditional route" and achieved great things.

Funding is a numbers game, the Francorp team told me. It's about how many phone calls you make, how many networking breakfasts you attend, how many presentations you give, how many doors you knock on. It's about follow up and more follow up. I was a willing learner at the hands of this group of seasoned professionals, so I followed everything they said. I started a written log, as Don had suggested, and kept track of every call, every word uttered by either party, the time, day, phase of the moon and important points I wanted to recall. Of course, being me, I went a little overboard and turned my call log into a diary with photographs of presentations and attendees, colorful crayon markings to depict red-letter days or successful calls, and photocopies of emails from key potentials. I also created a vision board with dollar-sign markers, pictures of people shaking hands to seal a deal, and affirmations depicting my triumphant fundraising efforts.

Making your own Vision Board is another great way of focusing your intent, and creating a tangible reminder of what you want.

Within three months, I had commitments of up to $350,000 from investors on the east coast. Of course, it was not without a lot of toil and, at times, some real anxiety. I flew from California on several occasions to meet with interested parties. I traversed the snow-covered streets of the northeast, schlepping my presentation boards and suitcase full of CosmiKids décor and trinkets. At the elegant Renaissance Hotel in Pittsburgh, the site of my first funding presentation to 10 investor hopefuls, I was so happy to have both gears—spiritual and business—on full throttle. Funding can be a real nail biter because you know that bringing your idea to the world isn't going to happen without it. I stayed present during these presentations by checking in with my intuition for guidance; this quelled my nervousness, gave me a quiet assurance that everything would come together, and helped me to take the focus off the end result and relax into the moment. I would say that the more we go within in this way, the freer it leaves us to embrace whatever comes up.

At $350,000, I was halfway to my target. Then I hit a wall. One day, return phone calls were rolling in and the next, they had screeched to a halt. In presentations, I was met with blank stares. For some reason, my list of interested potentials had suddenly started becoming less interested.

I completely believe in "divine supply" economics—i.e., that the universe is infinitely generous, that there's enough goodness to go around (and around and around), and that abundance is our birthright. It's exactly what we teach children about prosperity consciousness and self-sufficiency at our Roads to Riches discovery station. One day I happened to be talking with a friend. When I mentioned that I was halfway to my goal, she playfully challenged me to remain authentically committed to my path of spirit-based entrepreneurship and raise the remainder of the money solely through anchoring intentions, focus, accessing the emotions and detaching from the outcome.

"Well, that's fine when we get down to conducting day-to-day business but I'm trying to attract qualified investors here!" I heard myself saying in response. "This part is stone cold business! Until this part happens, nothing gets done!"

Suddenly, a light bulb went on.

So that's why everything had stalled!

Raising money through intention setting had worked many times for me already in small ways. Sometimes, the appearance of the funds I had wanted to attract had been quite obvious, as in the case of the $8,000 I had been offered during my Boston lunch—exactly the amount I had needed at that time (and hadn't even voiced the need for out loud). Other times, the process hasn't been that cut-and-dried.

Suddenly, it hit me that universal abundance doesn't distinguish amount. In some ways, I was applying finite thinking to the force of nature, which of course is infinite. The Law of Attraction states that the universe and everything in it is composed of energy in motion. Everything that exists vibrates. Add to this scientific fact the one that says energy cannot be created or destroyed, it can only be transformed, and suddenly I could see that *all energy that is, was and ever will be already exists in some form right now*. So, we cannot really destroy or get rid of anything. We can only transform it into something else. And since each of us has access to "everything that is," and since money is simply another form of energy in our material world, this meant that whether I intended $500 or $5,000,000, the formula was exactly the same.

The universe really is a massive candy dish brimming with good and plenty for everyone.

In the light of this epiphany, the only question that remained was "How good am I willing to have it?"

From a spiritual perspective, I was being asked to apply this same mind-set to the $350,000 price tag dangling in front of me—the cost of bringing my baby into a much larger playground. Here I was, living these personal development techniques in every aspect of my life, so why not give it a go with raising the second half of my working capital?

So that's exactly what I did. I jumped off the ledge of limitation into a sea of possibility. If nothing else, it would be a fun experiment. It's the same thing we teach kids. We have them fish for wishes from our Bridge of Imagination and blow bubbles to detach from the outcome. Whether it's wishing for an iPod or raising millions of dollars, the process is the same. And it's really that simple. Even a child can do it.

For a cosmic split second, jumping off that ledge was frightening because I knew it required total surrender. "What ifs" rose up from the depths of my psyche. I knew the formula worked . . . but, but, but . . . what if it didn't this time, what if it took longer than anticipated, what if I looked foolish in others' eyes, or my own eyes?

I stepped back, took a deep breath, and witnessed myself going through the anxiety. The first thing I saw was that this was a pivotal growth point. *How could I espouse the principles of divine supply—ask and you shall receive—unless I walked my talk through how I choose to fund the very project that was built upon these metaphysical tenets?*

It was time to go within once more and determine what I could do energetically to facilitate this second half of the process. From that moment on, I stopped calling potential funders. I scheduled no more presentations. Now I was completely on my own. Just me and my faith in the universe.

The next morning, after checking email and brewing a cup of chai, I set up an altar in my bedroom with Lakshmi (the Indian deity of riches and abundance), my lucky looks-like-the-real-thing million dollar bill, some blessed red rice that was left over from my Feng Shui graduation ceremony and a red envelope with my newly stated intentions folded neatly inside. For good measure, I placed a three-inch round mirror beneath the envelope to reflect and enhance my intention in the black sect Feng Shui manner. Later that day, I sat in meditation with sincere gratitude for all the lessons, struggles and successes I'd enjoyed thus far. I felt it was important to acknowledge everything that had led up to this point, for they were all crucial steps in bringing the funding process to fruition—at least, the first phase of it. That evening, I wrote intentions in my faithful binder then verbalized them. As I spoke, I felt in my heart the tingling feeling of accomplishment that I would experience once the monies were in our corporate bank account. I put my signature to the written intentions, closed the binder and placed it on my bedside table. Like a child on Christmas Eve, I lay down to sleep with butterflies in my stomach and a calm assurance that wonderment would greet me in the morning.

Do I make it sound too easy? Simply write, state, feel and build an altar? Well, believe it or not, it really IS that easy. (And sometimes even easier!) At the same time, it's important for me to say that I believe these techniques have brought results based on a sincere and solid foundation of personal development over the years of my life.

For many years, I had impatiently pushed and promoted my ideas, even forced them. Now, with a more refined spiritual awareness and first-hand knowledge of an easier way to accomplish most anything, I had every motivation to completely step out of that mentality. I wanted to live in complete faith that my fundraising goals had already been met. So every day that week, I stayed focused on the tasks at hand, knowing that the company "already had" a solid financial base. Even in my off-work hours, I'd feel in my heart that our investment monies were in place. Any time a thought arose that was anything less than optimistic and aligned with my desired outcome, I'd reaffirm my intention to raise a million dollars. (I had upped the target from $700,000 on the recommendation of a dear, astute friend, whom I lovingly call Esther the Investor, who cautioned that I would need three times more than I thought, and three times longer in which to raise it. In tribute to her, I added that $300,000 cushion—Why not? After all, intentions don't need to be capped—but I didn't feel the need to ascribe to Esther's idea that it would take longer.) I intended that this second half of funding would arrive not through toil and uncertainty but with ease, grace and joy.

> 🦋 Act as if!

Karmic Lucky Strike

It was an otherwise ordinary southern Californian day—exactly six days after I had initiated my "second half" funding ritual. As I was driving along the freeway, I looked at my car's GPS screen and noticed something I'd never seen before: blue dollar signs dotted along the route that I was traveling. I blinked hard then laughed out loud.

"Now that's abundance! Thanks Lucille!" I said, using the pet name I'd given to my navigation system.

Perplexed and amused by this, I stopped my SUV at the first opportunity and took a photograph of the dollar-sign-dotted screen. Intellectually, I realized that those signs indicated ATM machines or banks located along the route, but my inner voice chimed in that this was a cosmic wink from the universe that money was on its way. I sat in gratitude for a few minutes then turned the key in the ignition to continue on my way to meet my colleagues. Lena, Tammy and I were in worker-bee mode in our make-shift offices at Lena's home. Tammy was debating whether to use pink or gold adhesive strips on our new session packet. Lena suggested going with whatever felt right. I had just taken a spoonful of key lime yogurt and was now typing on my laptop when my cell phone rang.

"Hello?" I answered. On the line was a voice I hadn't heard in years—an attorney that my former husband and I had engaged way back when. My stomach did a flip.

"Are you sitting down, Judy?" Dan said. I placed the yogurt cup squarely on the desk and slid onto the couch.

"What's up?"

"Remember the $40,000 investment you and Larry made in a start-up company ten years ago?"

"Yea, I remember, but to be honest, Dan, I haven't kept track of it. What's going on?

"The company is being sold."

"What does that mean?"

"It means that you will very likely be coming into a serious amount of money in the very near future."

"What?" I stood up, accidentally tipping over a two-liter bottle of spring water.

"We don't have the exact numbers yet but your return could be in the millions."

My mind went blank as I tried to fathom Dan's words. Was I hearing right? Was I dreaming? Something in my being knew immediately that this was my miracle in waiting, the payoff for my faith . . . and it was far, far grander than anything I had imagined.

How good was I willing to have it? How good, indeed! Within one week, the amount of money that I intended had presented itself in a way that I would never, ever have guessed. At the time, it seemed so far-fetched that I wouldn't have believed it was really happening, except for my trust in the power of surrender. Truly, I hadn't considered that this windfall might occur—especially to the extent or within the timeframe that it had. I had nearly forgotten about the potential personal payoff from this investment. Of course, there was always the possibility that it could happen someday. But from the outside looking in, there were many intricate variables involved in that company's situation that could have led to alternative outcomes that weren't so positive. That's why it hadn't really crossed my mind before. This windfall felt to me, and still does feel, like a karmic lucky strike. The universe had conspired with a precision that had allowed myriad details to converge as they did, when they did and how they did. The only thing I was in charge of was who I chose to be in those moments as they transpired. And, just as I had in preceding moments of uncertainty and seeming chaos, I chose gratitude.

For the next several days, I allowed myself time and space to dwell in thankfulness and reverence for the powerful, far-reaching principles of intention-setting.

I now had nine passive (yet passionate) investors who resonated with our mission, the needed working capital *and* the freedom to bring my concept and way of doing business to market. As majority stockholder, I had the usual reporting and fiduciary responsibilities to shareholders with the added delight of being in the driver's seat of a company that mirrored who I was and what I had dreamt of for so long. It was more than . . . well, not more than what I *could* hope for but more than what I actually *had* hoped for. That's the power and majesty of the universe. To this day, I'm in awe at having been given the resources that enable me to be the steward of this idea.

With all the necessary funding now in place, I was eager to forge ahead with developing all aspects of the company—and I continued to use intentions to focus my vision and allowed the Law of Attraction to propel me towards it.

Angels on the Streets of Brea

The time was now right for me to transform CosmiKids from roving festivals to an independent, permanent operation with its own location. I also needed to start hiring employees, building company infrastructure and securing accountants, IT support, a marketing staff and ad agency to help define and brand our emerging company image. Within a few short weeks I packed up my Bridge of Imagination, Scrumption Machine, Spiral the six-foot dragon mascot, our beloved Cosmic Girl poster and a handful of CosmiKids coloring books, and set out to find new digs. By then I had two part-time staff and 20 loyal volunteers—people who had supported CosmiKids through facilitating the experience for the children, as well as contributing ideas, physical labor and marketing services. From 2003 to 2005, we had staged many authentic play experiences for children and parents all over southern California—from San Diego to Carlsbad, to LA County and Whittier. We had worked out of Lena's big, brown family van, offering 90-minute, day long and three-day CosmiKids festivals. Anywhere from a dozen kids and up to 400 parents, children and community minded visitors attended these play sessions. They were rich years of research and development. Through these experiences, we had learned what worked and what didn't, and we constantly refined and reworked every aspect.

Lena was in charge of managing the festivals, training our facilitators, curriculum development and eventually had an early hand in our décor redesign. She was in her element with the children and volunteers. I interviewed staff and attendees, manned the stations as needed, interacted with children and facilitators and garnered feedback from parents. I encouraged Lena, along with her friends and collaborators Tammy and Uran, to make the stations more portable, more compact and more cost-efficient. Lena did a monumental job of whittling down a big vanload and an entire truckload of CosmiKids décor, furniture, signage and accessories into a box of materials for us to transport to New York and North Carolina for our CosmiKids festivals at Bard College and weekend retreat in the Blue Ridge Mountains. While Lena and her trusty team loved the organic, easy flowing experience as it had always been in the early years of their neighborhood festivals and were quite happy to keep it as they'd always known it to be, I became increasingly focused on building a profitable, sustainable business. Lena and staff lived 80 miles north in Orange County and I hoped to locate an office and prototype location somewhere nearby. Lena and I spent hours walking the streets of Whittier, Santa Fe Springs and Tustin. Nothing seemed to have my name on it. Then we happened upon Brea. I immediately loved its look and feel—a mixture of New York's Soho and Pittsburgh's Shadyside. The streets were clean and the sidewalks literally sparkled. As we stood in the town center, I mentioned to Lena that

I'd set a specific intention to find a cozy, affordable little loft in which to live, something central to everything and hopefully close to our soon-to-be office. I'd never been to Brea and didn't know anything about available real estate and rental costs. Talk about the Law of Attraction! At the very moment I spoke this, I looked beyond Lena to a building that bore a sign saying Birch Street Lofts. And there was a gentleman, who I later learned to be the building manager, coming through the entry gate. A month later, I moved in. But we still needed office space.

One day as Lena and I met for lunch on Brea Boulevard, she suddenly stopped dead in the street.

"Look!" She exclaimed, pointing to a six-foot bronze angel sculpture on the street corner. The angel was poised for action, busting through what looked like a wall of boxes.

"Hey, she thinks outside the box, too!" I joked. "Let's make her our company mascot!"

Long story short, our new guardian angel's outstretched hand just happened to point directly to a building on Brea's main street . . . our new office location. It was a small space but we made the most of it. Our artist-in-residence, enchantress of color, ambassador for peace and curriculum developer, Uran, painted magical wall murals. Rainbow-hued beaded curtains reflected sunlight through the windows. A cool, ice blue-leather couch and furry, neon pillows perfectly accented the space and delighted the eye from the entry door. It was the Law of Attraction at work once again: we intended to furnish our new digs in a lavishly cosmic way with a very modest budget.

And so it was.

So, 2005 was a very good year; one in which divine supply showed itself in forms too numerous to count, and returns on our intentions—our valuable new ROI—became the norm for us, rather than the exception.

As we set up shop in Brea, another round of the magical mystery tour was about to commence. Along with it would come another huge challenge which would bring with it my next level of personal growth. This one, I didn't see coming.

14.

"Shift Happens" No Matter What

Such is life—just when we take the training wheels off, something comes along to make us feel wobbly. If there's one thing we can count on, it's that change will happen. And in this new paradigm of inner work and outer rewards, it's just as certain that "shift happens"—maybe even more so. From an enlightened perspective, there's no such thing as "business as usual"—at work or in life—because when we make a commitment to becoming our best possible selves and aligning with our purpose, situations arise that give us opportunities to do just that. But they're not always pleasant. That's why, as I've repeated many times in this book, it's not about *what* happens to us, it's about *who* we are going through it. In the end, all we can do is grab the handle bars, find our own balance and rely on ourselves to steer towards where we want to go.

By summer 2005, things were getting wonderfully intense. We had set up our first company office, ramped up staffing, worked with Francorp on our franchise model and produced a cool DVD for potential franchisees, fine-tuned operations, and begun readying for our first ever franchise trade show. Once more, I'd never worked so hard, stretched so far, or had to trust so much. I loved (almost) every aspect of it, and was grateful for the incredible opportunity. I knew where we were headed, and it was what I'd always dreamt of. With informational requests from around the globe, Don felt the time was right for us to make our debut in the franchising marketplace. We signed up for the International Franchise Association's West Coast Expo at the Los Angeles Convention Center.

All told, CosmiKids now had 30 people at that time in various parts of the country (including New York, Chicago, Pennsylvania and California) collaborating with us in preparation for our debut. Our ad agency had done a stellar job of creating award-winning collateral materials and a polished web presence for the show. With Cesar Zapata, our exhibit designer, at the creative helm and Guillermo Ascanio overseeing the design of our miniature model for display at the show, our look was polished and cutting edge. Our New York publicist, Gerry Harrington, was busy weaving together national media relations and interfacing with Gail, who handled PR for us on the west coast. In Chicago, we contracted the services of Skyline Trade Tech to design our booth and coordinate logistics. Lena, Mark, our director of sales, and our local team prepared sales materials and made sure no details fell through the cracks. I was busy coordinating the set-up on site.

All the usual marketing, sales and operations decisions were taken care of, and—as usual—they were overlaid with our conscious business practices. We set clear intentions: for qualified, soul-aligned franchisees, for the franchise sales closing process to go smoothly, for an amazing CosmiKids buzz at the show, for our post-show franchise receptions to be standing room only, and for our relationship with Francorp to further deepen. As we packed up our expo supplies for transport to LA from Brea, we put good thoughts and loving energies into each box.

As Lena and Cesar had worked together throughout the preceding months, we had continued to set our intent that positive thoughts were being infused into the very fabric of whatever we were creating. We would imagine in our mind's eye the joy on children's faces as they sat in our colorful pyramid tents, and the look of interest on prospective franchise buyers' faces as they watched our DVD or listened intently while we answered their queries about a totally new play space for children. We would envision all that we intended then let it go and be open to receiving whatever the universe had in store for us.

We did all of this because we believe that, ultimately, what lies beneath the savvy marketing, professional image and thoughtful content also speaks volumes. That energy, while intangible, is extremely powerful, and I am convinced that people are gradually becoming more aware of the essence behind words and deeds. Indeed, in more and more businesses, authenticity is becoming the new TQM (Total Quality Management). As is probably quite evident by now, I have long believed that each aspect of how we conduct business should pass a sincerity test of sorts. Does it really add value to people's lives? Can this product or service really fulfill its promise? Does it uplift or degrade society? Does it truly "do no harm" to others and the planet? Is this triple bottom line of "people, planet and profit" driving

Remember— whatever you intend to create is likely to affect other people. So always take the greater good into consideration and include it in your goals.

us or are we eschewing the environmental and social for only economic gain? These questions may not have mattered as much in the past, but they are now becoming increasingly important as our consciousness expands, causing our inner "bullshit meter" to become more attuned.

Fair Trade Show

Going into the West Coast Expo, I was concerned that we didn't yet have a profitable location up and running. Not to worry, Francorp said, you're selling a first-in-its-category concept but the brick-and-mortar part of the business is not unlike any other franchise. We would offer them the innovation, proprietary curriculum, field-tested Stations of Discovery and training methods, and Francorp would help us deliver the business systems and operations, just as they'd done for thousands of successful franchises in the past. With expert coaching from Francorp, my team and I had our CosmiKids sales pitches down pat:

"It's like the one-room schoolhouse, jazzed up and supercharged for the millennium!"
"It's an amusement park for the soul and interactive children's museum rolled into one!"
"It's a first-of-its-kind, pint-sized personal development center for the whole family!"
"It's a playground for the kinder, gentler, leaders of tomorrow!"
"It's an empowerment salon for the modern community!"

On the opening day of the show, I was asked to speak at Francorp's kick-off breakfast for about 40 clients. From there, I scooted off to meet my team at the hotel restaurant across the street from the convention center. As we fueled up on fresh juices, wheat toast and scrambled eggs, we covered all last minute incidentals—right down to making sure everyone had gel insoles in their shoes.

"Look at the time!" Mark said. The show hadn't officially opened but we had been advised by Francorp to arrive early. Of course, everything was set up and ready to go, we just had to man the booth. As we high-tailed down the main conference floor and round the corner to our exhibit lane, who should we see but Mr. Poker Face himself—tapping his foot and gesturing pointedly at his watch.

"Glad you all decided to join us," Don admonished. I felt like a kid being scolded for tardiness on the first day of school. But under his stern veneer, I could see a glimmer in Don's eye of the proud parent introducing his debutante.

Three exhausting yet exhilarating days of chatting it up with hundreds of people from all over the world—whew! God bless whoever invented those gel insoles! All in all, it was a great experience, and we came through with flying colors. Our intention to create a CosmiKids buzz was realized within hours of the show's opening. The first day, we received accolades from the International Franchise Association higher ups when they unanimously awarded us "Best in Show" for the freshest booth design. Not bad for newbies! Lured by our silhouetted artwork against vivid colors and the upbeat tempo of our looped DVD featuring the Black Eyed Peas' infectious song, *Where is the Love?* we captured the attention of passersby long enough to invite them into the space to view our miniature model and munch on freshly baked cookies packaged with inspirational messages.

Our intention to garner attendees for our franchise receptions in the months to follow manifested, as well. From that inaugural show (and another we attended months later on the east coast), we received lots of qualified leads. But it soon became apparent that only a small percentage of these were actually ready to purchase a CosmiKids franchise. As we further qualified those individuals, we discovered that a smaller percentage still fit the exacting requirements to become our very first CosmiKid franchisee. That franchisee's personality, integrity and resonance with the CosmiKids' philosophies were of the utmost importance since they would become the poster child for our business model. A soulful twinkle in their eye was just as crucial as seasoned selling tactics or solid business abilities. After a few months of well-attended receptions, we still hadn't signed any franchisees. So our primary intentions to attract the exact right franchisees at the show and smoothly close our first few deals didn't manifest.

Why not? I gave this a lot of thought over the following months. During that time, we discovered much that we had needed to learn, refine and apply to our special niche. If we had been selling an ice cream, mailing services or printer cartridges franchise where there is no public learning curve, we probably would have sold some locations. Those businesses are like a peanut butter and jelly sandwich—mostly everyone has tasted one and would agree that it's a winning combination, whereas CosmiKids is more like my favorite concoction of PB and banana. (Yes, we are a little bananas!) After all, we're layering traditional business, franchise and education structures atop nontraditional perspectives and new paradigm philosophies. It's a creamy-nutty-sweet mash of all these things, and unless you've tried it, you'll never know how good it can be.

Some have said that our trade show experience was premature, that we should have waited until we'd had a profitable location up and running for a few years before attending as an exhibitor. Granted, a lot of time, money and resources had been spent on that show. It would be so easy for me to boo-hoo the fact that the outcome wasn't something like "five franchises sold". Does that mean we made the "wrong" decision? As always, it comes down to the belief that if one is aligned with one's purpose and has faith in one's abilities, *whatever* happens is divinely correct. Second guessing is useless because what's done is done. When we entertain regret, we're living in the past. Success, like everything else, is in the present. And compassion isn't something we just have for others; it's something we must afford ourselves, as well. So, instead of bemoaning our fate, I stayed focused on the many good things that had come out of that experience and gleaned whatever valuable lessons I could—not the least of which was that it gave me even more confidence to keep moving ahead. I knew that the right franchisees would eventually be drawn to our concept and new paradigm business model, and I was determined that when they arrived, we would be fully prepared to greet them.

🦋 *Don't let yourself get derailed by regrets or comparisons.*

As word continued to spread about CosmiKids as a franchise opportunity, we connected with more enthusiastic and qualified leads from as close as Santa Monica and as far away as Dubai. I was particularly upbeat about a young Miami couple, Samantha and Roberto Montero, whom Don initially met and had given his blessing.

"Sam's the real deal," Don said. "She's got the enthusiasm, the smarts and the work ethic to bring your concept solidly to the east coast. She'll be the Hispanic Judy Julin!"

Sam was so gracious and endearing by phone. She shared that she had worked as an attorney until retiring to start a family, and that Roberto was a senior executive with American Express. I flew to Florida for a visit and immediately knew they were a perfect fit for CosmiKids. Even though their being on the east coast was a bit of a stretch for our first franchisees in terms of cost efficiencies, Sam's passion for making a difference with children, her spiritual sensibilities and her commitment to new ways of supporting our youth were more than evident. She had already canvassed Miami for retail locations. They spoke of long-term plans to open three franchises in south Florida and purchase the rights to Mexico. As I left the next day, we hugged and kissed each other on the cheek to cement the deal. Her two small boys, wide-eyed, adorable and golden from the sun, watched from the back seat of the car. We agreed that she would be sending me a check for the franchise fee as soon as Roberto returned from South America, and that she would come out to California for training in June of that year.

Then shift happened—for CosmiKids and, more importantly, for Sam and her family. The following week, she called in tears. Their precious little boy had just been diagnosed with a life-threatening medical condition that would necessitate special treatments for at least nine months. The Montero's put everything else in their lives on hold. Their sweet, sun-kissed child is now doing much better. We've kept in touch and still both hold the light of intention that Sam will reign as the Hispanic spokesperson for east coast CosmiKids.

When Dreams Diverge

Then shift happened—again. This time, it seemed to come right out of the blue. Yet, in retrospect, there had been signs. Small things that Lena had been doing leading up to the expo: less time spent in the office, last-minute meeting cancellations, mounting disagreements with consultants. One day during the middle of an executive team meeting, she tearfully resigned, saying that she didn't concur with the direction of the company. I was shocked. (*And I'm supposed to be conscious and aware? Ha! How come I hadn't known this was going to happen?*) Does our human nature cause us to dismiss or reject that which we would rather deny? In this situation, the clues had hit my intuitive sensor but I had chosen to ignore them. I hadn't wanted to entertain for even a second the thought of CosmiKids without all of the players on our enlightened simpatico dream team intact. Everyone was saddened by this sudden announcement and, at the same time, I admired the courage that it took for Lena to voice her truth. As much as she loved CosmiKids, it wasn't matching *her* vision for *her* life. She had come into our company as the owner of her own small business and had discovered while working with us that she still had a passion for being a self-made business person in her own right.

When a handful of us subsequently met to construct a suitable exit package for Lena, she further announced that two of her colleagues (whom she had introduced to the company) would be leaving with her. It was a tremendous blow; one that would essentially leave us with no one to lead sessions and oversee curriculum development. I later learned that one member of the trio in question actually had no intention of leaving; she continues to this day as a loyal, valued executive member. As a stockholder, Lena will hopefully someday further benefit from her time spent with us. For now, she has returned to her busy life as a devoted parent to four wonderfully gifted kids, and running her own enriching sessions for children.

Notes from the Abyss

When reality set in, I fell into a funk. I mean this reality: Hundreds of thousands of dollars invested. No franchises sold. Key people leaving. Revenue trickles, rather than streams. Decisions, decisions, decisions. Vision and envision and revision. *Do I need all this frustration and turmoil? What the hell am I doing? I could be leading a simple life, tucked away in a tiny cottage somewhere. I could focus on spiritual pursuits, maybe play a round of golf here and there. It wouldn't take much in the way of resources. I'd grow my own food on a backyard plot of ground, have friends over for herbal tea, and live off love offerings from hosting chants and meditation circles.*

Doesn't that sound like heaven? The devil on my shoulder was seducing me. *Forget all that "change the world" baloney. Who cares? And who do you think you are, anyway? PLERK, my ass! That corporate stuff will surely get the better of you. Just play. Come on, baby, bang on the drum all day. Come on!*

For several hours, I was beguiled. I lay on my bed fantasizing about this golf-and-leisure life that I could have.

It didn't take long for the fantasy to begin feeling hollow.

The problem was that it lacked the very thing that feeds me on a deep level: the desire to build and run a sustainable, environmentally sensitive, highly profitable, values and integrity-driven, multi-national organization that impacts the way we educate our youth in a powerful and positive way. Abandoning this dream would mean abandoning myself. And with several valuable people gone, I was already full bore in the abandonment department.

Slowly, I watched as my mood turned into one of self-righteousness. "I started this venture alone and by God I can do it alone again if I have to!" I yelled to no one in particular.

But that too isn't me. I live for connecting, collaborating and being with people. I thought about how much I had loved spending time with our dream team. I already missed them in my life.

Then I started to feel angry. *Man! I did my best to support them, compensate them well financially, and acknowledge their contributions. I gave them my trust, my heart, my love!*

Whew! I was taking this way too personally. I knew that I was really just mad at myself for wanting so much out of life. Sure, I could live on herbal tea and love offerings if I had to, but the truth was I didn't want to. I was made to live large and dream big.

Of course, key people were going to come and go during all phases of the company's development—especially if I was encouraging co-workers to always follow their soul's urgings. My charge was to continue to learn how to support their decisions and not take them personally, but rather, to bless their contributions and send them on their way with love and good wishes. Shining their light elsewhere didn't detract from CosmiKids any more than shining my light with CosmiKids detracted from what anyone else was doing. The point is to just keep shining.

So that's what I chose to do.

Within a few days, I had pulled myself out of my funk, and was starting to feel back on track again.

Onward and Upward
I awoke to the sounds of cow's mooing in the distance, and birds singing outside the window. I was in the country, and what a delight it was, after living amidst California's urban landscape for three years. Sandie was living on five sprawling bluegrass acres in Kentucky with her boyfriend. During my brief segue into the emotional abyss she had invited me down for a dose of gal-pal support.

The sound of birdsong seemed to wake me from my slumber—literally and figuratively. As I opened my eyes and stretched on the guest room featherbed, ideas suddenly started springing to mind about how to reorganize the company and roll forward. I reached for my laptop, fluffed some pillows for back support and started typing. The dissolution of our dream team had apparently created a vacuum of upward momentum. Ancient feng shui teachings state that when we clear things out, it creates space for new things to come in. It's important to remember that not all massive clear-outs are ultimately negative. In less than two hours, a full-blown plan had emerged. I hit "save", closed my laptop and met Sandie downstairs for a good, old-fashioned "cuppa" tea—the panacea to all ills, so many of my British friends tell me. We had talked for hours in our pajamas about our aligned dreams and desire to work together on that which we love—namely, empowering children and parents. I was anxious to get back in the saddle and this time I had a feeling that Sandie would be riding right alongside me.

My respite over, I returned to Brea, brimming with creative energy. Next on the CosmiKids agenda: hosting a Hollywood premiere for an up-coming documentary that I was to be featured in (more about that later in an upcoming chapter); devising a CosmiKids Discovery Tour; developing retail products; revising staffing considerations to bring on new hires as necessary; and scouting for a storefront location to field test our newly developed Stations of Discovery and—finally—enter the marketplace for real.

15.

Into the Twilight Zone

"I'd love to work with you," this stylish Asian woman had said to us while visiting our West Coast Franchise Expo booth. Kim was pretty, outgoing, two parts cool sophistication and one part razzle-dazzle. And she seemed very determined to work with CosmiKids. After several calls to our office following the show, we agreed to meet. A former law student, Kim spoke fluently about her work with children's organizations and her wish to do meaningful work with a company like ours. Enthusiastic and bright, she led a vegan-yogic lifestyle and was employed at the time with another child-oriented franchise company. Her intentions seemed genuine and we were pleased that this person had appeared out of nowhere when we desperately needed someone special. Note the operative words here: "desperate" and "special". In my haste to get all the balls rolling with our reorganization, I rushed to hire her to direct our Discovery Tour. We soon discovered that Kim was special all right, but not for any of the reasons we had initially thought. Ouch! Looking back, I can see that I had allowed my impatience and neediness to override my failsafe intuition. How human of me! I should have taken time to ground myself and align with my higher state. (But it's all divinely perfect, right?) Yes, Kim certainly entered my life for reasons far beyond leading Circle Time with our little ones.

After the dream team debacle, I had made the intention to become more adept at setting boundaries, speaking my truth and honoring red flags when they popped up. I vowed to communicate in the moment whenever my internal guidance told me something was amiss, and I was determined to learn to view others more through their own eyes, not mine. Obviously, I've needed more than one or two semesters on this lesson plan, as I keep getting retested on it. So now, along came Kim.

Scripting the Next Phase

Months prior to meeting Kim, and just before our company move to north Orange County when our dream team was still intact, we had decided to make a splash on the LA scene. I had no idea how we could penetrate such a dense, rich community where lots of cool events happen all the time. Working with the Law of Attraction once more, we were continually amazed at how small miracles seemed to occur almost daily. For example, in mid-2005, I had received a call from a friend, Donna, who was affiliated with a documentary that was being made about Indigo children and their special gifts. She needed a location near Laguna Beach, some children and adults to interview and a CosmiKids festival to film in real-time action. I was thrilled to have CosmiKids featured in a documentary that showcased our mission to empower the special children of today, and I immediately arranged with my dear friend Linda to use her house high up on a hill in Laguna. Its magnificent gardens, waterfalls and crystalscapes provided a perfect backdrop.

Six months later, CosmiKids was featured in *Indigo Evolution,* which documented claims of extraordinarily intelligent, psychically sensitive and spiritually evolved Indigo children. This concept had been receiving prominent coverage in major media such as *The New York Times, USA Today*, CNN's "Anderson Cooper 360" and Diane Sawyer on ABC's "Good Morning America." The film explored the meaning behind the growing evidence that more and more children born after 1970 seem to be displaying special psychological and spiritual attributes such as acute empathy and intuition, as well as very high intelligence and self-awareness. These nonconformist, bright children not only seem to be born knowing that they have a purpose; they also appear to know what it is and how to pursue it. Many indigos featured in the film have become acclaimed artists, poets, musicians and even peacemakers.

When I learned that CosmiKids would be featured in the film, we decided to make the most of our good fortune by sponsoring a public event. We ran the numbers and determined that the publicity we could generate for our brand would be worthwhile and lasting. Perhaps this could be the splash we were hoping to make? I was ready to take a chance, regardless. We staged a Hollywood premiere and co-hosted it with Sandie and *Children of the New Earth* magazine, her online evolutionary parenting publication. A prime example of Return on Intent, we magically were able to rent on short notice one of LA's most celebrated venues, the Silver Screen Theater at the Pacific Design Center in West Hollywood. We planned to follow the movie screening with a panel discussion featuring the film's co-producer/co-director/my new buddy Kent, as well as nine panelists, some of whom had been featured in the movie, ranging from child development/enrichment specialists to authors, psychics and school administrators.

Jan Tober and her business partner, Lee Carroll, were credited with shining the spotlight on the Indigo phenomenon through their groundbreaking books *The Indigo Children: The New Kids are Here* and *Indigo Celebration,* in which many well-credentialed educators and psychologists, as well as parents and caregivers documented their own experiences with Indigo kids. Lee and Jan did a wonderful job of presenting Nancy Ann Tappe's original research on Indigos. Just to fill you in on a little of the very interesting background to this phenomenon, back in the 1970s, Nancy had started documenting a difference in the color of the auras of many new born babies. Nancy has a medical condition called synesthesia, in which two neurological systems become crossed and the senses get reversed. This means that in addition to seeing auras (energy fields around the body), she also can smell sounds and hear sights. Having worked in China and taught at the University of San Diego, Nancy did extensive research and ultimately published a book in 1982 called *Understanding Your Life Through Color,* in which she reported that after 1970, about 80 percent of babies being born had indigo-colored auras and that this color equated quite specifically to certain characteristics and some rather highly developed abilities. As of 1990, about 90 percent of children being born had a lot of indigo color in their auras. As it happens, indigo is also the color of the third-eye chakra, an energy center inside the head located between the eyebrows. This chakra regulates clairvoyance, or the ability to see energy, visions and spirits, as indeed so many Indigo children seem able to do. Without Nancy's seminal work and Jan and Lee's pioneering efforts, no one would have even heard of Indigos, yet none of them had been invited to appear in the movie, which many people agreed was a gross oversight. Sandie felt that including Nancy and Jan on our panel and showcasing their contributions would be a well-deserved tribute, and I wholeheartedly agreed with her.

On the day of the premiere, Sandie gave both Jan and Nancy an eloquent introduction and had them stand to be recognized. From my vantage point in the wings, I watched them graciously accept the rousing applause from a packed audience. Jan's face softened and tears welled in her twinkling eyes. I became a little mushy myself. I was thrilled to see them receive the acknowledgement and accolades that were rightfully theirs.

We had arranged to videotape that discussion for potential distribution through various avenues. To make the event even more fun, we had also organized a post-show reception with good wine and food, author signings, gifts for all attendees and goodie bags filled with prizes.

Everything was proceeding really well, and we were looking forward eagerly to our first big Hollywood event when—yep, you guessed it,—more "shift" happened.

I've mentioned the phrase "shift happens" several times to make a point: it never ends, so we might as well get used to it. That's the charm of embracing process; there's always something more to hug because, in a very real sense, we are *always* attracting change to reorient us towards our intentions and purpose. No future outcome will eliminate this—not wealth, fame or social status. I'm learning that self-mastery is an on-going, ever-present, never-ending process—and so worth it. As the *Tao Te Ching* states, "Mastering others is strength; mastering yourself is true power."

I Can Do This Standing On My Head

With Lisa, our moderator, nine months pregnant, we thought it would be wise to have a back up person on hand in the event that she should go into labor. Earlier that week, our second in line, who was a professional speaker, had suddenly had to go out of town. With just two days to go, we looked around for a substitute. Since Kim seemed pretty confident and was willing to step in, we felt adequately covered. As it transpired, Lisa did go into labor. Thankfully, she'd had time to coach Kim sufficiently well for us to have confidence in Kim's ability to pull it off.

"Not to worry," Kim reassured us brightly before the event. "You know I've had acting training. I can do this standing on my head."

And handle it, Kim certainly did. In fact, she did everything *but* stand on her head. Trouble was, this was a professional panel discussion that required a serious, professional, and capable moderator who knew how to behave, how to segue graciously and professionally between speakers, and how to elicit information with intelligent, thoughtful questions. And what did we get? (Oh no, whatever you're thinking, believe me it was far worse than that!)

Ta-dah! Big cymbal crash! Kim leaped lithely on stage. She looked fantastic. Unfortunately, the perfectionism and professionalism she had displayed during her coaching phase had been overtaken by a hyperactive-bordering-on-manic stand-up b-a-a-d comedy routine, with the occasional soft shoe shuffle thrown in for good measure. And every single long drawn out moment of Kim's narcissistic performance was being caught on a film that we had been planning to package and market to parents who were eagerly awaiting this valuable information!

Oh . . . my . . . God! I couldn't believe my eyes. *Where exactly did Kim say she had done her training?*

Horrified, I glanced across at Sandie. Sandie was looking back at me with an expression on her face that told me she was somewhere between tears and laughter.

Please, tell me this is not really happening, I mentally telegraphed a plea to Sandie.

I could tell by the look on Sandie's face that she'd got my T-mail.

Oh yes, it is. Her answer came swiftly back.

How do we get her off stage? I shot back silently.

Too late for that, Sandie's expression said. She was right. There was nothing we could do.

Our nine panelists, including me, sat quietly as, like a stage struck amateur who has suddenly been given her 15 minutes in the spotlight, Kim took full advantage of the situation to make herself the center of attention.

Silently, I prayed that once she moved from the podium to the moderator's seat her common sense and professionalism might kick in.

Thankfully, once the dialogue got rolling with the panelists, Kim seemed to calm down a bit. Our panel was brilliant and audience participation was robust. But of course the damage had been done. The moment the panel discussion was over, Gail quietly informed me that an editor from a top magazine had been so appalled by Kim's posturing she had walked out. I gulped and kept my chin up. Thankfully, the reception was well attended by journalists, authors, health practitioners and a few celebrities, as well as the general public, most of whom were too polite to mention the Kim gaffe. So it wasn't all bad: we garnered lots of good media coverage, a lot more LA folks now knew about CosmiKids, and the movie went on to be shown around the world. To this day, people still mention seeing CosmiKids in that film.

But what to do about Kim?

After much thought, I decided that here was another primo chance to walk my talk, honor red flags, set boundaries and stand in my truth. Isn't it lovely how the universe artfully creates ways to keep us honest? After the panel discussion, I simply thanked Kim for her contribution but said no more at that point. With the harried nature of event day and hundreds of people around, I decided to wait until we could talk one-on-one. Besides which, I wanted to hear the feedback from others in attendance. ("Get another moderator" was our only complaint of the day). That evening, we never got the chance and the next day, I was scheduled to go out of town for 10 days. Not wanting to wait that long, I wrote Kim an email. It's not the most personal mode of communication, especially for delicate situations, but I wanted to articulate my honest feelings and have it in writing for her to digest before we spoke in person. Since we were going to have to edit the panel discussion for public sale, I thought it would be a good idea to invite her to participate in that task. If most of the reel with her talking was going to end up on the cutting room floor, I wanted her to know why. I also explained that I wanted to make sure we correctly matched people with their talents and strengths. I invited Kim to share her truth with me, as well. *Perhaps I had asked her to do something before she was ready.* Overall, I felt that my email maintained a positive tone, with a little constructive criticism delicately thrown in. Kim eventually responded with a thorough and gracious email, and I breathed a sigh of relief.

Single, White Female
Thankful that Kim was being so reasonable about the affair and feeling confident now that her behavior had simply been a momentary aberration fueled by last minute nerves or some such, I left town in a fairly happy and relaxed frame of mind. Little did I know that while the vaudeville act might be behind us we were now heading full pelt into . . . *The Twilight Zone.*

I arrived back from the east coast, eager to get on with interviewing and hiringour first full team of Vibes (the name we coined for our staff) for our upcoming launch, which was now just months away. Out of the blue, one evening, Kim called to ask if she could come over to my new Hollywood apartment to watch an HBO special on my TV. Sandie was in town again, and we had a business dinner that evening, so I gave Kim my key, the entrance card to my building and a set of written instructions on how to use the TV. In the middle of dinner, my cell phone rang. It was Kim. Judging by the way she was speaking, it seemed that she was in some distress.

Concerned that there was some kind of emergency, I spoke as calmly as I could. "Could you slow down, please Kim, because I really want to help you but I cannot make out what you are saying."

"How do you work the freakin' TV remote? I'm missing the show!" she screeched impatiently.

I calmly suggested she read the directions I had given her, as I was in a meeting. At that, Kim got very angry and hung up. *Hmmm....I thought... that's very odd behavior from someone who's a guest in my home.* We arrived back at the apartment that night to find the TV blaring loudly, and Kim stretched out on the sofa as if she owned the place, *in my bathrobe.* When she didn't look up or offer any greeting, I walked over to her and said hello.

Without taking her eyes off the TV screen, Kim casually announced, "I'm doing my laundry. Hope that's okay."

A chill ran through me… it was like watching a single-white-female scary flick.

"Could you please turn down the TV?" was all I could think of to say. She shot me an irritated look then grudgingly turned the volume down a notch or two.

Stunned by her behavior, I didn't know what else to say, other than "Well, please lock up when you leave, okay?" And with that, I went to bed.

At 3:30 in the morning, my cell phone rang.

"Did I wake you?" Kim asked.

"Are you kidding me?" was all I could say, half asleep.

"Did I wake you?" She repeated.

I said what I was thinking. "Kim I have to get up at five thirty!"

"Oh. Did I wake you?" It was a most peculiar phone call, especially at such an ungodly hour. But I was in no mood to stay on the phone a moment longer. I hung up.

Kim's odd behavior that night (coupled with some other incomprehensible incidents) prompted a conversation with our ops director about the need for regulatory personnel write-ups and a face-to-face conversation as soon as possible with Kim. She had accumulated three strikes against her now–with the early morning phone call, her unprofessional behavior at some recent trade shows we had exhibited at, and her seeming inability to understand the urgent nature of certain vital tasks. I had been willing to write off the movie premiere debacle as a blip on the radar screen of her internal psyche because she had seemed to take my constructive criticism reasonably well. Or had she? Could her latest antics stem from some underlying anger at my calling her on her inappropriate stage behavior? As I began to recount all the red flags that had quickly surfaced, I realized that there was no way I could allow Kim to continue to disrupt the smooth-running of our organization, especially now that we were so close to our grand opening. We would be nuts to have this woman as location director at our highly visible first location, but there was no one else to be found. I was feeling the mounting pressure and the clock was ticking. I took a mental step back, breathed, and did my best to reframe the situation and see what options arose. Maybe this was divine timing for Kim's departure. After all, through her dysfunction, she had allowed me to learn about red flags, speak my truth, set boundaries and trust my instincts. Should I be thankful or angry? It's always a choice. I had to trust that all would be provided for.

Lori and I scheduled a private meeting with Kim the following Wednesday at our Brea office. We planned to find out why Kim had acted the way she did over the last weeks, go over the points about her behavior that were unacceptable, and give her written notice of her dismissal. We wanted this exit interview in hopes of finding out the disconnects that led to her poor choices. We had also hoped to retrieve all of the important files and documents that she had in her possession, including details of all the Vibes she had been interviewing. That meeting never happened. For all intents and purposes, Kim disappeared from the face of the earth... along with all of our new hiree files, valuable documents, the keys to my loft and my building entrance card. And in fitting with her making an exit from my life that was as dramatic as her entrance into it the day I met her, Kim made off with the car I had allowed her to use while her own vehicle was undergoing repairs.

When I dialed Kim's phone, it went straight to voice mail. Several weeks later, I received an email from her with no explanation about her disappearance and a cryptic hint of where she'd abandoned my car. It was finally located on the basement level of a parking garage in West Hollywood, unlocked. How it wasn't stolen a second time, I'll never know. After spending two dreary hours with a sweaty but patient tow truck driver on the lower 5th level of a 110 degree parking garage, my car was finally towed back home. And you bet I had the locks on my apartment replaced.

To this day, I haven't again laid eyes on that Asian jewel who later became one of my most treasured teachers on the road of life and new paradigm business practices.

I've reflected on my time with Kim in order to understand why on earth someone would choose to act the way she did—not only to her employer but to someone whom she had said she regarded as a like-minded soul on a similar path of spirituality. This incident really stood out in my mind as a queer, troubling curiosity *and*, as always, a chance for some big learning on my part. I wanted to take advantage of it by learning what I could and then move on. Yet one more red flag in this instance was hidden: Kim's incongruous behavior obviously had psychological underpinnings. As with anyone else, I'd supported her in ways that not many employers would. Should I stop being that way? I don't think so. I would rather lose a hundred cars and loft keys than change who I am and how I choose to express myself through the creation and management of my company. But I've learned that I must remember to make decisions from a place of balance, confidence and trust, not desperation and neediness. Instant success requires constant vigilance of our emotional state and always "checking within" for a gut reaction. Our intuition is the truest gauge of red flags seen and unseen.

In retrospect, the whole Kim incident was just one more turn on the merry go round. At times, I've wanted to jump off the carousel and passively watch the horses glide up and down from solid ground. But in the end, the lure of happy Wurlitzer music always draws me back onto the platform because I'm one of those people who are not content to simply stand on the sidelines watching the ride. I want to be on it.

Every time "shift happens," it reminds me of what I've written into our CosmiKids principles: that having faith in our own abilities means we can *always depend on ourselves, no matter what happens or what others may do.* As the Tao Te Ching further imparts:

> I have just three things to teach:
> simplicity, patience, compassion.
> These three are your greatest treasures.

> Simple in actions and in thoughts,
> you return to the source of being.
>
> Patient with both friends and enemies,
> you accord with the way things are.
>
> Compassionate toward yourself,
> you reconcile all beings in the world.

If this philosophy of compassion for the self and others that I want children to know in their core is really essential, which I believe it is, then when applied to any of the stories outlined in this chapter or in this book, it certainly takes the edge off the drama. Moments of doubt may make me dizzy and cause me to step off the ride every once in a while, but I'll always jump back on the horse and enjoy the big spin.

16.

Flow with the Go: Finding Neverland

L ooking back on everything that had transpired in the previous twelve months—from our move to Brea and trade show debut to the departure of several key people to my subsequent move to Hollywood, and our film premiere and the antics of one bemused co-worker—there's no question that 2005 was a year fully lived. Successes and lessons galore! As 2006 dawned, it was time to assess all that had occurred and make adjustments for the future. Fact: we hadn't sold any franchises to date. Fact: we needed to open a temporary prototype play space in a retail locale so we could test the workability of our newly designed stations, as well as our operations, training and retail methods *and* so that potential franchisees and the general public could see a CosmiKids center in action (and hopefully generate a revenue stream from it). And now for the optimism part: this prototype space would be no ordinary space, it would be the grandest cosmic experience imaginable in one of the world's most desirable retail locations. Yes, I believed this could be a reality, and very soon.

Now that we had sufficiently tested our activities and methods on a smaller scale in San Diego and areas surrounding LA, it was time to step it up a notch. I believed wholeheartedly that CosmiKids would be received best if introduced in a high-profile, media-rich arena. Because we were pro-posing a never-before-enjoyed concept for children and parents, I wanted the whole world to know about it right from the get-go. Staging our movie premier that January at the Pacific Design Center further inspired me to move towards the epicenter of Hollywood. I loved the hubbub of Tin-seltown, the larger-than-life personas of the people who work there—not just entertainers but the whole entourage of business professionals that supports them. Everywhere I looked around town—in coffee shops and restaurants, on the streets, at neighborhood farmer's markets, in the dry cleaners or grocery stores, at gallery openings, while waiting on a velvet divan in the lobby of The Chateau Marmont for a lunch appointment—I saw artists, agents and producers striking deals; their conversations about "possibility" perked my ears and further stoked my fire. Even the star-studded sidewalks spoke to me, each one a reminder of other ordinary people who had followed their bliss, offered their talent to the world, and will be forever remembered for it. A desire to align CosmiKids more solidly with these energies of dream-building and chance-taking steadily grew inside me. Hollywood signified the same motto that CosmiKids offers to children: dream big, shine your light and dance to your own beat.

So I began my quest to find the right birthing station for our prototype location, which we decided would be fashioned as a POP-UP venue. As our chief designer Cesar Zapata pointed out, POP-UPs had become popular in New York and Paris as keen opportunities for high-end retailers to make a splash in an area, capitalizing on its out-of-nowhere appearance and novelty of entrance into a marketplace. For me, it meant that I could impact a larger area and say hello to more people with fewer long-term financial worries. But I didn't know where to begin locating 3,000 square feet of cost-efficient, visible, easy-access store frontage with a temporary lease. Los Angeles was foreign territory to me. I knew zip about the commercial real estate market there, other than the fact that it's exorbitantly expensive—if you can find available space at all in the most sought-after neighborhoods. Oh yes, you bet I'd be working with the Law of Attraction on this one.

After having traveled on foot to every possible retail venue, I was given a lead on a reputable real estate broker who was booked solid for months but was willing to talk with me informally about my needs. He was gracious and helpful, but unavailable. By then, our beloved design guru, Cesar, kept saying in his cute Colombian accent, "Judy, you simply must find a proper space for the prototype location! I cannot continue to design an interactive experience for children in thin air!"

I continued to trust in the always-on-time universal overlay and reaffirmed my intention to find the right person to assist in my search. Sure enough, a recommendation for another broker came through a friend that very day. Good thing, because the real-world clock was ticking. Our monthly franchise receptions in Brea had resulted in many interested potential franchisees waiting to see the CosmiKids prototype firsthand. I wanted to be able to show them something spectacular soon but Cesar couldn't complete the prototype design until we gave him an actual space configuration. After weeks of scouting for locations with the broker, we came up empty. Nothing seemed to fit our need for a short-term, reasonably priced, high visibility retail location. With our options running out, I suggested we check out a place that a co-worker had mentioned. She lived one street away from the world famous Hollywood & Highland Center and believed it would be the ideal place for our launch. The broker called the center's leasing agent and she agreed to show us the only available space on the property. I was in awe of the architecture of this world famous building and the hustle-bustle around it. What a fantastic location! In those moments, it seemed like a pipe dream—how could it all work out in terms of availability and, yikes, leasing cost? I followed the agent into H&H with an inner certainty that CosmiKids would land there and Cesar's stratospheric design elements would more than do justice to this amazing commercial space.

Then we entered the retail unit. My heart sank. Yep, there was a reason it was so "available". It was dark, hidden and in need of much repair. When I learned that it was formerly a bar, I declined. Not good "predecessor energies," as Feng Shui teaches—meaning that whatever or whomever previously inhabited a space leaves energy behind which could, in turn, adversely effect the current occupant.

With nothing else to look at, we exited the building. The sun was setting over the Hollywood hills as I stood with the broker and leasing agent near the popular stone "casting couch" sculpture, on which tourists line up in droves to have their photo taken with the Hollywood sign as a backdrop. As my associates said their goodbyes, I pondered what had happened that morning before leaving my loft. I had clearly set intentions and knew in my gut that today would be the day that the absolute perfect space would present itself. It would be on the first level of the shopping mall, with high visibility and affordable rent so that passersby the world over would see our space, experience the stations and tell others about it. It was so clear in my mind.

The ring tone of my Blackberry snapped me back to reality. It was Cesar, again. I put off his call because I had nothing to tell him—not yet. Just then, my eyes began to focus on the red walls behind where the leasing agent was standing.

"What's in there, behind that red wall?" I asked.

"Oh, that's a temporary exhibit hall," the agent said. "It's currently featuring Italian wedding dresses."

"When will it be vacant? What's the square footage?"

"I've got to run, I'll get back to you tomorrow," she promised.

"But wait!" I said anxiously, my heart beating faster and my feet tapping quickly along in my second-hand Pradas. Nonetheless, she continued walking towards the elevator to her office as the broker waved goodbye and headed in the opposite direction. I felt pulled, pressured and tired from the long days spent planning our launch—and we *still* didn't have a place to make our debut to the world.

Ugh! I thought, *there's got to be a better way.* I quickly summoned my tenacious spirit.

"Kristen!" I called out before she stepped into the elevator, figuring I'd give it one last shot. "I know you're in a hurry and it's late, but I would just like a few more minutes of your time to clarify a few points." Maybe I sounded desperate or maybe when she looked down at my over-sized men's surfer shorts, worn denim vest and sparkly pointed shoes, she felt a kinship with my fashion sense—but in any event, she did an about face and gave me a warm smile.

"When exactly can I call you?" I inquired after taking a deep breath to collect myself. "Are you available by cell? I'd like to find out more about this location as soon as possible. You see, if I don't find a place soon, I'm up a creek without a paddle." Before she could answer, my cell phone jingled again. I knew it was Cesar and I knew what he wanted. I let it go to voice mail and looked back at Kristen.

"Judy, I promise I'll put this top on my priority list and get back to you first thing tomorrow morning."

"Okay," I acknowledged, still a bit deflated.

"You know, on second thought," she said, turning to look at the big red door to our left, "this space might be just what you're looking for." I smiled a big smile.

You guessed it. Behind that red wall was our space in waiting. We got it for a good deal because it was essentially a raw space with no lighting, bathrooms, A/C, flooring or walls. Once the beautifully ornate Italian wedding dresses were shipped back to the Italian Film Historical Society, we began leasehold improvements and that raw space came alive. It was ideal—on the ground floor of the very same building as the Kodak Theatre, home of the Academy Awards and "American Idol" finals,—above one of the busiest traffic corners in the country. Each year, tens of thousands of tourists worldwide come to that intersection to view the world famous hand and footprints of the stars immortalized in the cement outside Grauman's Chinese Theatre. A Darth Vader look-alike and other novelty characters walk around as packed Hollywood tour buses line up 10-strong along the curb. We would have invaluable street frontage and windows large enough for a 30-foot CosmiKids sign. Our space would be directly across from a gold-mine Starbucks and a trendy California Pizza Kitchen. Around the corner is the famous El Capitan Theatre, which was set to host Sesame Street Live during our launch month. It would be the perfect location—and, as it turns out, aha, the perfect timing.

So we began preparations to step onto the world stage for a fun-filled six months and give hundreds of children a 4,500-square-foot space in which to fully be themselves. Lots of exciting changes and growth opportunities were afoot—including our Vibe training, space installation and curriculum refinement. The following few months would be an amazing journey, with everyone doing whatever it took to gear up for the launch. In addition to valuable word-of-mouth advertising, having this prototype space would finally allow us to learn even more about each station experience, replenishment needs, staffing requirements, budget considerations, on-going training, sales efforts and franchise model implications. Clearly, a lot of work was ahead of me and I was excited to get started. But for one indulgent weekend after signing off on the lease, I wanted to hit the pause button, take a respite from work and bask in gratitude for everything that had occurred. With every fiber of my being, I was thankful for everything we'd accomplished thus far and even more so for what was to come.

17.

Leading with Grace

When our professional practice is a work of art, it doesn't matter what we choose to do but how we do it. At the fast food restaurants that my former husband and I owned years ago, I wanted the employees to see me not only mopping the floors along with the minimum-wagers but whistling while I did it. Why? Because even though I entered that ownership position in the oddest of circumstances, I chose to be fully in it, to bring my whole self to the task—and to treat my employees humanely. Realizing even during those uncertain days in my professional life that success is in the present moment, the optimist in me would say, "Hey! I'm makin' the fries and today they're going to be the best fries ever! Want fries with that? Of course you do!" Maybe my ability to find joy in the fry vat would rub off on those alongside me. I did it for myself in a way, but I also figured that I had a times-ten better chance of inspiring them through example than cracking the upper-management whip. Even if those employees quit, stole or still came to work with bad attitudes, at least I still had my integrity. Years later, I still feel this way.

Each Day, a New Reel
In a matter of months, one of my big dreams was about to become reality: the grand opening of the first CosmiKids prototype space in a retail location, smack in the middle of Hollywood. In that short time span, I would be handed, on a silver platter, many chances to live the words of the CosmiKids philosophy: *The more we believe in who we are, the more potential we see in ourselves.* This gives us increasing confidence and a sense of internal calm, even in the midst of calamity. And that is exactly what was to come in the following few weeks for all of us at CosmiKids as we approached our public launch.

When Kim had originally been appointed as director of our new play space, we had naturally asked her to handle the initial screening of candidates for our Vibe positions. Now, here we were, three weeks before Vibe training was scheduled to begin, and not only was Kim nowhere to be found, but all the details of the candidates waiting to be interviewed had vanished right along with her. I was immersed in all details related to the design and installation of the space, along with ongoing franchise sales.

Since panicking wasn't going to solve anything, we all decided to take a deep breath and simply take each day as it came. First, we needed 15 full- and part-time Alpha Vibes, and a director—fast. I had also just brought into the fold a new operations consultant, Lori, who hit the ground running and, along with Mark, grabbed the reins and scrambled in the most convivial way to recruit a new director to replace Kim. The strongest candidate was a woman that Lori and I had recently met at the Whole Child Expo in Los Angeles, where CosmiKids had been a vendor and co-sponsor, along with *Children of the New Earth Magazine*. Cathy was a colleague of our dear friend and expert videographer, Brian. He fully understood the CosmiKids sensibility, having worked on filming and producing video shorts, workshops and sound checks for us, so our ears perked when he highly recommended Cathy to fill our vacancy. Three days later, she stepped in as director and quickly brought to us many good people (most of whom still work with us).

It was a beautiful thing. In two weeks, we had 25 magnificent Alpha Vibes ready to commit two full weeks of their lives for training before our launch. They were all ages, races and backgrounds—and every one was an amazing individual. Some were retired teachers and disenchanted corporate folk. Others were actors, clowns, authors, public speakers and healing professionals. One was a 20-something son of military parents who'd lived all over the world. Another was a young woman who had already worked with children in Nepal and other remote parts of the world. We would teach all of these Vibes another new manner of being with today's children, and we'd be doing it in a conscious, caring environment. To this day, I marvel at how Mark, Lori and Cathy were able to wield their magic wands to make this happen.

But not everything was peachy. We soon discovered that Cathy was spiritual in a somewhat radical way. I never thought I'd hear myself say that it's possible to be "too spiritual" but working in this new paradigm requires a fine integration between flying to the galaxies and staying grounded in common sense. I mean, yes, we were getting ready to open a retail space in La-La land, but only in the colloquial sense. When Cathy began to combine her atypical way of looking at the world and hard-to-understand reasoning into her decision making, I started to get nervous. For instance, she spoke quite intelligently about the paranormal and extraterrestrial existences, and while I'm open to all belief systems, it was all a bit too much for us to digest in a business setting. Up went the red flags, once again: Cathy became ultra-protective of the energy in the play space. Yes, we understand the importance of energy because we live by the principles of quantum physics, as well, but she was like a mother wolf about it—on the prowl and ready to devour anyone who invaded her territory without permission. Cathy's psychic comments were unvarnished, pointed and, at times, downright insulting. She had several showdowns with employees. One nearly quit the company because of her and, just as devastating, she alienated our franchisee candidate. On the surface, this was the reason why that candidate did not become our flagship franchisee—it was all too much for her, too. On the flip side, Cathy's antics enabled us to view this candidate in moments of discord and disharmony. She handled it all poorly and, as a result, it revealed to us that she was not in alignment with the caliber of individuals we seek as our franchisees. After all, if you can't work through discord with adults, how are you going to handle it with children?

Now that it's all said and done, I have to applaud the many positives that Cathy did bring to the company at that time. We worked through most of this strangeness as we went along and, woo-woo aside, she brought commitment, patience, and a strong work ethic that got the job done in warp speed. She also was a tireless worker, never backing away from what needed to be done in order to have everything in place by launch day. Was it easy? Geesh, at times, it was quite traumatic, but in retrospect, it was also a great training ground for me in that each unexpected situation gave me even more cause to learn to stop, breathe, stay present, and count the successes each day had brought, rather than focus on what had not gone right. Instead of eroding my confidence, each "traumatic" moment tested my potential to handle disturbing situations and, in so doing, strengthened my resolve to lead my life—and even the company—with grace under fire.

Our Hollywood grand opening was just around the corner now, and I was determined to enjoy it to the fullest—with my sanity intact.

18.

CosmiKids Goes to Hollywood

It was June 2006 and at last the dream I had dreamed for 25 years was finally coming true: CosmiKids was set to debut its first retail test site at a fabulous location I'd only seen in the movies and on TV—the famed Hollywood & Highland Center. This may not seem like such a big deal but it was for me. Several hundred people had gathered along Hollywood Boulevard to watch The Honorable Johnny Grant, Hollywood's esteemed mayor, cut the ribbon on opening day. He was flanked on a red carpet by celebrities, city notables, beaming child stars, international media, business executives, child educators, well wishers, our company team—and me, with the biggest grin that had ever been on my face.

The timing was perfect. All eyes were on Hollywood & Highland's Kodak Theatre that week, with the *American Idol* finals in six days and the *Academy Awards* in two weeks. Across the boulevard, *Sesame Street Live* was packing in families; since we'd partnered with them to cross-promote events, every one of their attendees was invited to CosmiKids on show day.

The design of the play space went far beyond my wildest imaginings, thanks to Cesar's creative brilliance. For months, he and I had pegged away at every inch of the decor. I knew it inside and out. That did nothing to prepare me, however, for the impact of its magnificence in full regalia. It had the feel of walking into a cosmic, benevolent and very creative world— another realm altogether of discovery, entertainment and encounter. In the spirit of youth, the environment was kaleidoscopic, futuristic and highly adaptable. Through cutting-edge media integration of sound, video, lighting, and immersive multicolored, flexible scenery, the play space literally responded and interacted with children and others who entered it. Even the furniture, curriculum tools and Stations of Discovery—which are all minds-on, portable and interactive—were designed to allow children to customize and transform them as they please, and to empower them to create and express without boundaries. The whole atmosphere added up to a fun, safe and nurturing space that is personal for each child, like a womb of their own to explore at will.

As the weeks went on, the test site attracted the attention of individuals from all walks of life. Tourists were abundant, of course, as were show-biz folks. Dr. Robert Rey of the popular reality TV series *Dr. 90210* came to CosmiKids one day with his children to film a couple of episodes that aired a few weeks later. One afternoon, in walked a short-stature, bare-footed didgeridoo player offering his cheerful music; his instrument was longer than he was tall, and his eyes sparkled as he played. On another hot summer day, three saffron-robed Buddhist monks came through with an interpreter. All smiles and giggles, they joined in play with the children for a while, then bowed and blessed the space and went on their way. The play space was open seven days a week, eight hours a day. We had hundreds of children, teens, parents, healers, workshop leaders, teachers, tourists, entertainers, franchisee potentials, business leaders, philanthropists, movie crews, city officials, television executives, strollers, street performers and even a few pooches grace our space. As summer blended into fall, we staged innovative birthday parties, facilitator trainings, corporate team-building workshops, live theatre and musical events, movie nights, book signings and daily empowerment sessions for our pint-sized leaders of tomorrow. Compliments of a Kiwanis Club donation, local underprivileged kids aged five to 12 came during their summer camp and were entertained for hours each day. Their squeals of delight made *my* day.

Hollywood 9021-*Oh!*

I've always loved going to the movies and have had a lifelong fascination with Hollywood because of the "make your dreams come true" mentality that permeates the city. The Hollywood sign, nestled in the hills yet so apparent, symbolizes for me (and probably countless others) hope, possibility and wonder. I remember reading an article in which actor Jim Carrey said he used to sit right below that sign and visualize himself as a star (intention + attention = box office leading man!). Way back since the Kids at Heart days, I've always felt that Hollywood, more than any other locale, epitomized the philosophy that I wanted my company to inspire in young children: be your bold self, dream boundlessly, act fearlessly and shine your light like the glowing sun that you are! Or, as Actress Judy Garland once said: "Be a first-rate version of yourself; not a second-rate version of someone else!" And yet, for many people, Hollywood represents a negative connotation of plastic, shallow, self-obsessed, debauched, spoiled celebrities who can't stay in healthy relationships or out of rehab. Because the Hollywood rumor mill is so pervasive in our media-driven culture, this image of Tinseltown seems to be firmly entrenched in the mind of society. For this reason, I used to view my love of Hollywood mystique and glamour as a conflict to being a spiritually conscious entrepreneur who wishes to pass along simple, grounded, heart-based values to little ones.

That conflict was mostly put to rest once I began to mingle with, meet and befriend some of those same Hollywood stars and realize that they're no different than the rest of us—they just happen to be doing what they do in a very public arena. Like every industry, I've discovered that the entertainment business contains all types of people—including those who are genuine, gracious, goodhearted and not at all like the gossip rags would have us believe. Two celebrity moms, in particular, have truly won my heart. One is actress, model and author Jenny McCarthy. Jenny is so full of life, positive, spiritual, fun and generous—treating Sandie and I to lunch when we meet. Jenny, whose son, Evan, is autistic, has done so much to raise awareness of autism by detailing her journey and the discoveries she made along the path to helping her son without resorting to medications in her wonderful book *Louder Than Words: A Mother's Journey in Healing Autism*. She has also been so gracious and supportive of CosmiKids, speaking on our behalf, and gracing our H&H ceremonies as she helped to cut our opening day ribbon. To me, Jenny embodies the new paradigm of thinking as a parent. "I can't wait to see what this generation does," she confided to me one day. "It gives me such hope for the future. Imagine finding your life mission in first or second grade!"

The other thoroughly modern mom who amazed me was Emmy-and Golden Globe-nominated actress Sherilyn Fenn of *Twin Peaks* fame. Sherilyn's beauty (she has graced the covers of *Playboy, Harper's Bazaar, In-Style* and *Rolling Stone*) is only surpassed by her inner beauty and intelligence. Sherilyn is as real as a person can be. In fact, she calls herself "The One Who Pulls Weeds" because she does her own ongoing internal work, speaks her truth, calls a spade a spade, and commits herself daily to being the best that she can be. One day, Sherilyn and I were chatting about this dichotomy in Hollywood, and what she said helped me to further reconcile my spirituality-celebrity conflict. She spoke of several important mentors in her career who taught her about the true riches in acting and how to mine the gold in acting.

"One of my teachers early on said to me, 'You have a more important reason to be at an audition than to get the job'," Sherilyn shared with me. "He explained that it's very personal work *always*. Acting is about looking deeply at stuff—not figuring it out and demonstrating it but figuring it out *while* you're in the midst of reading your lines and connecting with whomever is across from you in that scene."

"That's a very different way of working than just memorizing and delivering dialogue!" I noted.

"Exactly. Even the word 'acting' implies pretending, faking. It's just the opposite. He said: 'What makes a star is the extent to which you're willing to reveal your soul'."

"*Very* cool," I interjected.

"Oh yes, and when I learned that about acting, I was so excited and inspired. It made me want to go into it more deeply. It really is that simple. Most people don't or won't do this—in acting or in life. They're not willing to reveal their souls. The actors who touch us are the ones who give a real personal story, sub-textually, through the dialogue—everyone watching the scene gets it on that sub-textual level and they have their own personal experience of it. It becomes engaging and you can actually grow from watching people's work. That's the ancient art of storytelling, period."

"So, it's about being authentic, which can be applied on the scale of life, as well." I said, to which Sherilyn agreed.

"Here's another example," Sherilyn continued. "A woman who I met early in my career said to me, 'I think you're trying to be who you think people want you to be. If you're shy or obnoxious or however you are *authentically*, if you can just be that, you'll be a person who directors want to work with.' She gave me permission to be myself and my very next appointment was with director David Lynch. I was shy and myself in that audition, and he ended up writing a role just for me in *Twin Peaks* that changed my career. It was amazing verification of how powerful we are when we're *real*. The teacher I have now once said to me, 'If you walk in the room to be seen, you're dead on arrival. If you walk in the room to see humanity, your own will arise.' So, it's about being yourself—in your work,

🦋 *Put your focus on seeing rather than on being seen. And be yourself, rather than what or who you imagine others expect you to be.*

in business and in life. Don't show up and be who you think they want you to be. It is okay to just be who you are—and that is when you will meet with success."

So, once I realized—partly through Sherilyn's words and friendship—that I could embrace Hollywood and my love of celebrity AND do what I'm doing professionally, well, I could almost hear the gods laughing. Living and working in Hollywood is perfect for me because I feel so alive here, so at home. I can embrace the energy of excitement and promise that's in the air and pursue my own unique passion. We all meet with success when we shun the naysayers and do what our hearts are calling us to do. As superstar Tina Turner once said: "The real power behind whatever success I have now was something I found within myself—something that's in all of us, I think—a little piece of God just waiting to be discovered."

And if you remember anything at all from these pages, I hope it will be this: you don't have to change who you are in order to be successful—no matter how you define "success". No level of success is worth that—unless, of course, you don't like who you are to begin with (in which case, no amount of fame or fortune or wealth or anything external can change that). I was reminded of the importance of being who I am (in a rather painful way!) when Sandie and I were out one weekend having fun trawling the vintage/second-hand shops along wild and wonderful Melrose Avenue. I was in my glory when I spotted a Goth-style mannequin in a window sporting a faux leopard-skin swing coat. The owner, a part-time drag queen in full dress, caught my drift and promptly set about accessorizing me in the spotted coat, with a 1950s red straw hat, sparkly sandals and a polka dot scarf. As we traipsed down the Avenue an hour or so later, Sandie laughingly drew my attention to my reflection in a storefront window.

"You know what, Judy? I think you look the epitome of 1950s style and wealth in that outfit. You should wear it to your meeting with the bank on Monday. If that doesn't convince them you're worth investing a few million in, I don't know what will!"

I giggled along with her as I imagined the raised eyebrows it would cause… then a hint of sadness welled up in me at the thought that once CosmiKids became a huge enterprise, I would more than likely be expected to dress conservatively at all times. *Would I still have an outlet to express the side of me that wants to be totally spontaneous? Or, would my non-conformist fashion sense and style prove totally unacceptable?* I inwardly lamented.

The next morning while making my bed, my back suddenly jolted in spasm. This had never happened to me before. I couldn't straighten up. When I tried to move, I felt an excruciating pain knife my shoulder blades. As I collapsed on the bed with a muffled groan of pain, Sandie appeared at the door.

"What happened?" she asked.

"I don't know." I winced. "I was feeling perfectly fine a moment ago. Now suddenly, I can't move. I don't know what to do."

"Okay, just breathe, and do your best to relax," Sandie said soothingly, as she instinctively started using her hypnotherapy and neurolinguistic programming training to calm me.

Several moments passed as I followed her instructions to breathe my way through the pain.

"Now tell me, what were you thinking of just before the pain struck?"

"I don't know… Nothing… I'm not sure…" I struggled to get the words out in between breaths, as I mentally replayed the last few minutes.

Hmmm… I was making my bed… as I reached across to retrieve a pillow on the far side, I was reminiscing about the fun we'd had the day before… brunch… chatting… shopping on Melrose Avenue… the conversation we'd had as I'd sashayed out of that dressing room, wearing the 1950s fake leopard-skin swing coat… Aaargh!

"That's it!" I blurted out.

"What?" Sandie prompted.

"Remember what you said when we were walking down the street, laughing at my reflection in the shop window?"

"Go on," Sandie encouraged.

"Well, that's what I was just thinking about." I confided slowly. "Sandie, you know what my biggest fear about success is? It's that I might be forced to change myself in some way in order to be taken seriously. I mean, my eclectic fashion style might seem perfectly normal on Melrose Avenue or Hollywood Boulevard, but it might not go down too well with the franchisees, investment bankers and shareholders that we could be mixing with once CosmiKids really starts taking off. You know how important being free to express my creativity is to me! My color sense and design style…

the way I love mixing unusual and original things together…these are all part of the way I express myself… What I didn't tell you yesterday when you made that joke about wearing my faux leopard skin coat and red hat to tomorrow's business meeting, was that the prospect of having to start molding myself into someone else's idea of what's considered acceptable in the corporate world… well, it gave me a huge twinge of concern."

Sandie sat quietly as my mind began to slowly acknowledge and explore the thread of connection between the mixed emotions of delight, regret and apprehension that had accompanied the memory of our experience on Melrose Avenue, and the crippling pain I'd experienced a few moments ago.

As the seconds passed, an amazing thing started to happen. Slowly, the pain in my shoulder blades and back began to relax and subside. Suddenly it all began to make sense: something deep within me had gone into resistance…the pain I was experiencing was connected to the sharp twinge of fear I'd felt at the thought of compromising my unique style and sense of whimsy for the more conservative world of business. I didn't want to temper my eccentric nature for anyone. I'd long ago accepted that the only way to live was to be fully and completely true to myself in everything I did. In fact, I believe it's imperative that I always bring my fullest, creative and imaginative self to the fore in my business life, or else my authenticity will be challenged and my visionary possibilities would be compromised.

"Wow! Talk about getting a perfect demonstration of how strongly our bodies reflect what's going on in our minds and hearts," I said, shaking my head in awe, relief and gratitude.

"Yup," Sandie agreed. "It just goes to show you that it only takes one part of us to feel ill at ease for our entire system to become totally out of alignment."

Thankfully, my little reminder about remaining true to myself had been mercifully short, sharp and to the point. Within a while, I was able to get up off the bed and go about my day with gratitude, a deeper understanding and new respect for what our bodies can tell us… if we are willing to open our hearts and minds and heed its innate wisdom.

Of course, as with all important life lessons, we invariably need more than one reminder before these universal truths sink in all the way down to our muscles.

As we moved through the next few months of our critical research and development phase at the Hollywood and Highland Center, I remained blissfully ignorant of the fact that I was soon to receive an even more compelling reminder of the importance of *always* remaining true to myself—no matter the cost in terms of pain or provocation.

Here We Grow Again

I had anticipated that planning our launch at Hollywood and Highland, building our brand, field testing our programs and hiring the amount of staff we needed would require a pretty sizeable budget. I had also anticipated that, by the time we opened our permanent site we would have sufficient franchises sold to help balance outgoing expenses against incoming revenue. Unfortunately, we had yet to sell a single franchise. So, even as we proceeded full blast ahead with our R&D experience at Hollywood and Highland, I privately pondered the potential consequences of our financial reality if the sales we were anticipating didn't occur soon.

As luck (or synchronicity) would have it, along came a friend from the east coast riding a white horse and offering a means to interim financial solvency. I'd met Courtney when she had attended our CosmiKids space at the Chopra Center years earlier. She told me that she loved what I was doing, and shared that she too was in the business of educating children. As we had got to know each other, I came to admire Courtney a great deal. She was smart, ballsy and savvy in business—having single-handedly built her award-winning centers throughout the northeast.

"She has the killer instinct," Don commented upon meeting her—something that we both knew was just not in my nature.

With her loving yet assertive, can-do personality, Courtney rode back onto the scene like a female gladiator, offering to hook me up with an esteemed financial consultant who had the wherewithal, she said, to assess our situation and provide us with some sound recommendations. This consultant had years under her Texan belt in all areas of finance and corporate downsizing, and an impressive list of companies she'd served. I scheduled for this consultant and her east coast colleagues to fly out and meet with us. Courtney spoke about receiving CosmiKids shares in return for introducing me to investment angels who could potentially act as additional funding sources. I agreed that combining CosmiKids' spiritually sophisticated curriculum with interactive technologies and an award winning, literacy-based educative model could be masterful, and Courtney and I began to explore a formal agreement for working together and sharing resources.

We had also entered into talks with a third company to form a partnership that would allow us to take advantage of key tax incentives for child care build-outs.

Within a month, everyone involved in this new collaboration was gathered at my apartment at Sunset & Vine, enjoying a kickoff dinner party before we got down to brass tacks the next day. At the party were various co-workers, friends and a few neighbors from my new apartment building. One was a filmmaker, Jeff, who had become quite dear to me. Earlier that morning, over coffee and oatmeal, I'd shared with Courtney that I felt a romantic attraction to this man. I confided how special he had become in my life and how much time the two of us had been spending together enjoying fine wine and late evening candle-lit dinner conversations. She listened intently as I shared my innermost feelings on this and other personal matters. I felt blessed to have her in my life.

That night, the party rocked with Marvin Gaye and Justin Timberlake on the CD player, good food and wine, and stimulating conversation about business, children's education and nearby shoe-shopping haunts. Busy being the host, I didn't notice at first that Courtney was getting really friendly hanging with my neighbor, whispering in his ear in between laughs and giving him her full attention. As the evening progressed, I watched with a growing sense of disbelief and bafflement as Courtney cozied up blatantly to Jeff in the kitchen. Judging by his smile and body language, Jeff seemed to be a willing participant. Later, as they headed toward the door, Courtney turned briefly to give me a smile. I didn't know what to make of it. Was it meant to be a signal of triumph? Or was she sending me a message of apology? Either way, it didn't really matter; for me, the party was over. I said a few parting words to her, yet felt disappointed, humiliated and betrayed—by both of them. I couldn't fathom why either of them would want to embarrass me so publicly. Everyone knew that Courtney was my house guest. And Jeff knew that she was both a friend and business colleague. Even if he wasn't interested in me romantically, I had thought he at least respected me as a friend and confidante. I wished he would have handled the situation in a more gentlemanly and discreet manner. As for Courtney… well, there was absolutely no excuse for her behavior; it was totally and utterly inappropriate.

As soon as I could, I brought the party to an end and bade everyone goodnight. As I got ready for bed, I felt like a teenager whose prom date has ditched her for another girl. *Why was this happening to me? And why was it happening NOW, when everything in my life seemed so tenuous?* CosmiKids was at a critical stage of its life; the expense and stress of our several-month-long sojourn at H&H, while absolutely necessary for research and development, had put a huge dent in our financial reserves. We still hadn't sold any franchises. Courtney and her friends had come to LA, ostensibly to offer their assistance in re-appraising some important aspects of the business, as well as to negotiate some kind of collaborative relationship with us. It seemed that all was turning topsy-turvy now, with this new shadow side of Courtney surfacing. In one fell swoop both my ego and my heart had been bruised, and the worst of it was I sensed there might still be more to come. As I lay in bed, looking up at the ceiling, the only comforting thought that occurred to me was at least it was better to find out now than to learn later the true nature of the people I had been contemplating getting into bed with—both literally and figuratively speaking. Yesterday, Courtney and I had been discussing the final points of a new business relationship, while Jeff and I (or so I had thought) were tentatively teetering on the brink of something a little more intimate than our casual, late night chats. Now, both these relationships had taken a surprising and unexpected U-turn.

The next morning, standing over a pile of dirty dishes in the sink, I didn't know what I should be feeling. On one hand, did I really have the right to judge Courtney's and Jeff's personal choices? After all, they were both consenting adults. On the other hand, there was no denying that the way they'd both behaved had been inelegant, insensitive, immature and downright hurtful. While the Irish in me kept exhorting me to quit the belly-aching, suck it up, and acknowledge that my personal feelings had no place at the negotiating table, another part of me kept reminding me that this attitude—and Courtney's and Jeff's behavior—was diametrically opposed to everything I personally believed in. I don't believe for a second that we can compartmentalize our work and our personal lives. Who we are in our personal lives *is* who we are at work, and vice versa—at least, that's how I feel we *should* be. As the Buddha said, "Who you are and what you do should not be a hairsbreadth apart."

Just then, I heard a knock at the door. I swallowed hard and opened it to find Courtney standing there, looking quite unrepentant. Judging by the mascara-smudged creases beneath her eyes, she'd had a very active night. With a tight smile, she brushed past me, remarking that she was heading to the shower and would be ready to leave for our upcoming meeting with her associates in 30 minutes.

I was so stunned, I couldn't think of a single thing to say.

An hour later, still trying to work out whether the quirk of Courtney's mouth had been a smirk of satisfaction or a wry expression of repentance, I steeled myself to remain calm as I seated myself at the table opposite Courtney and her financial *wunderkind* consultant. Yesterday, we had been cordial, business-focused, and keen to arrive at prudent financial decisions about how to move forward. Today, everything was different. Somehow, the two of them had managed to line themselves up side by side across the room from me. I didn't like the arrangement, and couldn't decide if this had been managed deliberately or if it had simply occurred by chance. Either way, I felt that this had become less like a collaborative business meeting, and more like a formal interview; one in which I and my abilities had already been judged and found wanting. I had the uncanny sense that all we were waiting for was someone to unroll a proclamation and pronounce my sentence. But I was determined that, regardless of the conclusions Courtney's team had reached, I was going to comport myself with as much dignity and grace as I could muster.

The meeting kicked off with a stiff little discussion about their observations of various activities at the Hollywood and Highland Center, then quickly moved on to the all-important financial issues. In the middle of analyzing the profit and loss statements, the Texan suddenly leaned over and drawled in a somewhat patronizing manner:

"You know, Judy, you should leave the running of your company to someone like Courtney. You're much too nice. Now, Courtney, *she* has what it takes to get the job done."

Stunned and insulted, my eyes flicked towards Courtney who was lounging quietly in her seat with her arms crossed over her chest and her legs encased in tight hip hugger pants splayed wide apart in a none-too-elegant pose. She had the decency to keep her eyes cast down, but if she was affecting modesty at the Texan's compliment, the effect was ruined by the shadow of a smirk playing at the corners of her mouth.

Looking back, I don't know how I managed to keep myself together. But from somewhere deep inside me, I managed to find the wherewithal to politely thank the Texan for her advice and move swiftly onto the next agenda item. All the while, my brain was firing off a million conflicting thoughts as a maelstrom of emotions started erupting inside me.

How dare they! The business woman inside me was outraged. While another more detached part of me was endeavoring coolly to assess *What was REALLY happening here?*

In truth, it was all so unexpected; I really didn't know what to think or how to respond. On the one hand, I was paying these consultants for their expertise, thus a part of me felt it was necessary I remain open-minded and accept their critique in as constructive a manner as I was capable of. At the same time, however, I was feeling both deeply wounded *and*, frankly, ambushed. *Was it possible that Courtney had been harboring a different agenda to mine all along?* I wondered. As I tried the idea on for size, mental Post-It notes started popping up in my consciousness, reminding me of several past incidents which, had I been paying proper attention, would have quietly highlighted some less than integrity-filled aspects of Courtney's personal character—like the time she had used our cornerstone company graphic and one of our ad slogans for her own business purposes without asking my permission, then denying it once I had brought it to her attention. From somewhere, an unwelcome thought poked at my consciousness: *Could it be that today's 'business' had actually been plotted, planned and scripted in advance?*

Courtney had always reminded me of the ex-pro WWE wrestler Chyna Doll, and now I was beginning to understand why. Suddenly, I was in the ring with my defenses down, and she was stronger, tougher and more capable—or so she and her companion were trying to convince me.

As the end of our meeting drew near, the alarm bells were ringing loudly in my head. Clearly, I could no longer trust that Courtney had either my or CosmiKids' best interests at heart. While I admired what she had accomplished in her life, I didn't *like* who she was or the way she did business. More importantly, I certainly wasn't about to *become* like her just to win the approval of a top-flight consultant and have them deem me capable of running my own company. Somehow, I was going to have to reach deeper inside than I'd ever reached before to find the courage to voice *my* truth about the situation that was now unfolding.

Before I had time to marshal my thoughts, however, the Texan dropped an even bigger bombshell.

"After spending several days reviewing every single aspect of your company, here's my recommendation," she said without a trace of emotion.

"Close the space immediately and put all staffing and cash outflow on hold. Then take some time out to regroup and reassess your market position. Once that's accomplished, we will then decide the best arenas to move forward in."

I was speechless.

Sure, I knew things had not been looking good. We had been bleeding money with no end in sight. Unsure where to turn, feeling alone and financially vulnerable at the time, I had brought in Courtney and her consultants in the hope that they might be able to provide some kind of panacea to the gloomy outlook that CosmiKids seemed to be facing. Courtney had held out a hand of hope to me, letting me know that she had the promise of funding, a link to financial strategists, a partnership plan for growth and a pipeline to big government dollars. Whatever I had been expecting to emerge from this weekend, it certainly hadn't included any of the scenarios that had unfolded over the past twenty four hours.

I had let Courtney into my life on every level—into my heart, my home, my life, and my business. And now I had to face the very real possibility that in doing so, I had allowed myself to be set up. *Had Courtney ever really wanted to co-create something wonderful for kids with me? Or had her real motivation been to fold our proprietary curriculum under her umbrella, and perhaps even replace my vision for CosmiKids with her own?*

To this day, I do not know how I managed to bring that meeting to a polite end. All I can imagine is that the survival instinct must have kicked in and triggered some button that pushed me fully onto automatic pilot. Somehow, in spite of the tangle of conflicting thoughts and emotions that were scrambling my brain, I managed to keep my dignity and act with restraint. But all the while, a little voice kept repeating in my head: *There's more to this than meets the eye. I need to get out of here. Go somewhere on my own. Thank goodness they are leaving town.*

My head was swimming. I needed some time alone to think; to digest the Texan's summary, and find some way to come to terms with the implications. According to her final assessment, CosmiKids was a failure on its own, and the only glimmer of salvation lay in joining forces with Courtney's company. The worst of it was, everything seemed to be pointing to the fact that the Texan might be right.

It took Sherilyn's unique style of tough-love for me to finally come to terms with my deep feelings of betrayal and mistrust of Courtney and all that she stood for. I had so much going on at the time that I was really at my wits end, about ready to crack under the weight of it all. I'd been hit hard on both counts, below the belt personally and in the gut professionally. I was just about at rock bottom, ready to throw in the towel completely, when everything came to a head. And I couldn't have picked a more public place. We were smack dab in the middle of the perfume aisle at the Saks Fifth Avenue store in Beverly Hills when I finally decided that I needed and wanted to tell Courtney exactly how I felt.

We had just finished a morning meeting when Sherilyn announced that she had an errand to run. Quietly, with tears welling up in my eyes, I had asked if I could accompany her. I really needed a friend, and it felt good to be with her, to have someone to talk it out with, someone to help me sort through my feelings and make sense of them all. As we passed through the glass doors of Saks, all the thoughts and feelings I had been storing up suddenly started to tumble out. I told Sherilyn how humiliated I felt at Jeff's behavior. I told her how stupid and small I'd felt when the Texan had informed me I wasn't capable of running my own company, and how I was even beginning to wonder whether she was right. As we turned the corner, Sherilyn grabbed my arm and brought us both to a screeching halt. Looking me squarely in the eyes, she said:

"Judy, that was a callous, insensitive move on Courtney's part. What a bee-y-a-t-c-h! You've got to call her on it and tell her how it made you feel. How dare she do that to you, at one of the most difficult times in your life, and as a guest in your home, nonetheless! How ungrateful and insensitive. What she did to you was a totally bullshit, low-class move and you know it! Quit trying to find justifications for her behavior. Start digging deep into how you *really* feel, and then go ahead and call her up right now and give her a piece of your mind!"

Then, as if it had been scripted, the clerk behind the make-up counter chose that moment to recognize Sherilyn. Shouting out her name, the clerk waved her arms excitedly in the air to attract our attention. Without missing a beat, Sherilyn shot back an exasperated, "Can't you see we're in the middle of something?" Then, with steely eyes, turned back to me and said, "Well?" I knew she was right. Mustering up my courage, I walked towards the shoe department, took a deep breath and punched the speed dial button on my cell phone.

"Courtney, I have to tell you how I feel about the way you behaved with Jeff," I began. When I had finished, there was a brief silence.

"Well, that's just the way I am, kid!" she said, in a completely dismissive, take-it-or-leave-it tone.

That was when I finally accepted that the chasm between Courtney and me had grown too wide and too deep for us to ever bridge again.

I later told her as simply as I could that as much as I wanted (and, yes, needed) for our deal to happen, I was still having a hard time reconciling us moving forward as business partners in light of what I perceived to be more than one severe breach of trust. Her tone in response was angry and defensive. I took a deep breath and held my ground, saying that I was by no means unappreciative of her professional support; I was just having a hard time with this personal matter of trust.

"Yea, and after all I've done for you!" she shot back. "I can't believe that you're so shortsighted and ungrateful."

Ungrateful? That word, and the way Courtney said it, stung my ears like a final, crushing blow. I felt my heart hit the mat. On every level—as a woman, as the child inside the woman, as a business person, as a trusting friend, as a dreamer of dreams—I had been KO'd. There was nothing more I could do but hang up.

I should have felt devastated. Instead, I felt strangely buoyant, as if a *huge* weight I hadn't realized I had been carrying had suddenly been lifted from my shoulders. Suddenly my mood lightened and I began to feel strangely empowered. In speaking her truth, Courtney had finally revealed her true essence. Yet at the same time, I could also see that on another, perhaps even more profound level, she also had been an angel in disguise. Courtney had brought in seasoned professionals to help me see my business brutally clearly. She had also helped to reveal Jeff's true nature. Of course, I would have preferred these epiphanous experiences to occur in a softer and gentler manner, yet, *it was what it was,* and I had grown and become stronger, both emotionally and professionally, from the experiences.

In the final analysis, Courtney's behavior enabled me to see her as the wise woman she was; one who simply chose to handle her life differently than I chose to handle mine. Which is, after all, what makes the world go round... each of us doing things our own way, with neither approach being any better or worse than the other.

Just when I thought things were beginning to calm down, I received a bill from the Texan for her consulting fee, which was substantially higher than the figure Courtney had assured me her friend would be charging. The only surprise was that I still had it in me to be surprised.

19.

Meltdown at Miramonte

A nd so began another "dark night of the soul" inward search to seek the answer to what I should do next.

Financially, emotionally, psychologically and spiritually reeling from my smack-down with Courtney, I once again collapsed against the ropes of self-doubt. This next round wasn't me against Courtney or her consultants. Nor was it me against the world. It wasn't even me against God. This round was solo.

It was me against myself.

As any fighter knows, shadowboxing is a brilliant training exercise. With no one to spar but yourself, and just a mirror to reflect back your every move, shadowboxing is a powerful one-on-none practice. It aids in the attainment of rhythm, agility, confidence, proper form, sure-footedness, adaptability and, perhaps most importantly, endurance. This is what I was about to learn. For the next few weeks, I spent most of my waking hours throwing punches at no one in particular, sparring an imaginary opponent that threatened to bring me down for good and end my dream forever.

I'd been tested many times before (as I'm sure we all have) because repetition is how we perfect our steps. I'd been to the edge of the abyss and questioned God as to why certain things have happened in my life. Yet something about the incident with Courtney and her advisors felt seismic. It rocked me to my very core. This time I was in the abyss itself, no longer questioning God, but myself. In fact, it felt as though *everything* about me had been called into question—not the least of which was me as an entrepreneur, and my new paradigm style of doing business. Courtney and her consultants had hit me where I lived. All of my dreams and plans, indeed *everything* I'd staked my reputation on, invested my heart, soul and money in, and pinned my hopes on had, in that last meeting, been laid bare in front of me. According to the Texan, I wouldn't make it as a business woman; I was too nice. The implication being: grow some gonads, girl, and maybe you'll get there. Oh, and by the way, not only is it okay to let this hardball ethic spill over into your personal life—it's mandatory. *Sleep with your friend's and colleague's love interest? That's just the way it is, kid.*

Maybe Courtney and her cohorts were right about me. Maybe their way of thinking was saner than my way. Maybe I didn't have what it took—maybe I was going under, and the word failure just means failure. After all, these consultants were paid to know about such matters, right? Maybe I should just grow some and become a bad-ass—or, turn the company over to someone who is.

Maybe. But I'm a lover not a fighter.

In that final phone call to Courtney, I'd had to summon up every ounce of my belief in what I was doing with CosmiKids, which was damn hard in the face of what I'd just been told about my company's financial picture and my supposed inability to run it. As far as I was concerned, that phone call had been a triumph, a success in its own right, because I had mustered enough nerve to confront Ms. Chyna Doll, heed my inner voice, speak my truth (my Achilles' heel resurfacing!) and stay in my integrity.

I had listened to my intuition, even as it had been telling me something I didn't want to believe: despite her giving nature, Courtney had *always* had her own agenda—which is fine, except that in my book, that's not true co-creation. I saw now that I hadn't wanted to believe it because the collaboration we had been planning would have solved a lot of big concerns for me going forward… The question was: at what cost? I had allowed myself to give away my power on many levels in those meetings, which is the last thing in the world I would consciously choose to do. Once I realized what I had been doing, I chose differently. I honestly had not thought that speaking my truth would bring both my friendship and my business partnership with Courtney to an end. But that's exactly what had happened.

Up until that fateful meeting with Courtney and the Texan, we had been considering extending our temporary lease at H&H; in fact, I had started to negotiate with the building manager to offer a "drop and shop" arrangement for the children of mall-goers. Many of the center's shop owners encouraged us to do this because they also brought their children by on a regular basis and thus knew it would be an attractive proposition for their customers. But now I had made up my mind to close the location, analyze how our six months had gone and take time to regroup, just as the Texan had recommended. As we approached the end of our lease, I scheduled a final luncheon to thank our executive team and vibes for their tremendous work. I did my best that day to remain upbeat, but I was exhausted, disappointed and, yes, strange as it may seem, even a little bit relieved—disappointed that we *still* hadn't sold any franchises yet relieved that the dollars would no longer be flying out the door with little in return. We finished our meals and I said a few final words of thanks to everyone, then the microphone was passed to one of our younger, teenage vibes. I fought back tears as her gentle voice came through the speakers. She thanked me and CosmiKids for the opportunity to work in an environment where she had felt supported, cared for and truly appreciated—and for being part of a company that had the vision to do something revolutionary for kids. After a few more gracious comments from the executive team, amidst cheers and claps, someone started playing The Black Eyed Peas' CD of "Where is the Love?" That did it for me. Aware that I wouldn't be able to hold myself together much longer, I said my goodbyes and snuck out the side door.

Time in the Desert

It was evident to everyone that the highs and lows of the past six months had taken a heavy toll on me. I was emotionally and physically drained. As Lori and Sherilyn helped me wind down operations at H&H and close the space, they turned to me and said, "You are going away somewhere to relax for at least a couple of days, Judy, and if you don't take time off to do this we will *make* you do it!"

Wearily I assured them both that I would look into it.

The next morning, I glanced wistfully at the sticky note bearing my grandest CosmiKids intention that I had pasted on to my bathroom mirror. Then I looked back into my own eyes. I had been PLERKing 24/7 for so long I'd lost sight of myself. *Had I been putting too much emphasis on this endeavor? Had I been fooling myself about CosmiKids? If this venture really was my mission in life, how come things weren't working out as I had envisioned? And now that H&H was closed, what should I do next?*

Somehow, in putting every ounce of my energy into CosmiKids, I had begun to lose sight of myself. I no longer knew who I was without it. I had given myself over to it too completely. It mattered too much. I had become too attached. Staring back at myself, I knew what I had to do; just as completely, I now had to let go. I didn't know what I would do next.

As luck would have it, Sandie just happened to be coming into town the following week. If anyone understood the impact of what I had just been through, it was she. I asked her if she was up to joining me for a few days R&R at a spa somewhere. "Absolutely," she said without hesitation. "Don't worry about a thing. I'll take care of all the research and find somewhere wonderful for us to go."

A few days later, we set off for the Miramonte Resort Spa in the desert community of Indian Wells, near Palm Springs.

As we drove toward the desert, I settled into the sinking feeling in my solar plexus. Slowly, the beginnings of an emotional upsurge began to quietly surface about everything that had transpired over the past year, perhaps the last six, and even the last lifetime or two—culminating with the past few days in which I had deconstructed the space at H&H. While Sandie napped during part of the drive, I slipped deeper into thought about all that I'd lived through since arriving in California—my beach prayers, rediscovering my dharma, aligning with the Chopra Center and delving more fully into Deepak's *Seven Spiritual Laws of Success*. Then striking out on my own in Brea, growing the company to four full-time and 20 part-time staff, coming into funding in that most serendipitous way, building the franchise business model, debuting at H&H and appearing in *The Indigo Evolution*. What was that all about? Where was it all leading? My intention remained the same: to build a new paradigm educational model for children that is a highly profitable business—sustainable, environmentally sound, global and operated with all the compassion-based principles that we espouse for children. Most mornings, while brushing my teeth and reading the intention pasted on my bathroom mirror, I had stared into that mirror from a certain angle and seen infinity. Strangely, in these past few weeks, the bright light of that intention had seemed almost too much to bear—like staring at the sun. Thinking about it now, it felt as if some aperture of hope inside me had reflexively closed. I couldn't think straight anymore. I couldn't think—period! My brain was too tired. Wanting to shake off all mental chatter, I turned on the radio.

"Who are you? Who, who, who, who?" the voice of Roger Daltrey of The Who screamed at me through the car stereo. *"Who are you? I really wanna know!"*

Hmmm, good question, perfect timing.

"Judy, how are you feeling? I mean *really* feeling…" Sandie gently probed as we strolled the grounds at Miramonte later that evening. Her soothing British accent seemed perfectly in sync with the cadence of our footsteps as we rounded a corner and came upon a lovely pool and waterfall. I told her the truth: I felt heartbroken, frustrated, defeated. As we stopped to dip our feet in the cool water, I admitted that I just didn't know what more I could do, or what I should do—and even if I had known what to do, I didn't know if I had the strength anymore to do it.

"You know what?" She responded quietly. "At times like this, the best thing to do is nothing," She paused for a few moments, and then continued: "Judy, you've always held fast to the belief in *being* versus *doing*. Maybe this is the true test of what needs to happen next. Do nothing. Just *be*. Shine your light and simply be."

"Ordinarily, I would agree with this, and I DO believe it, Sandie, but right now it all seems too simplistic. Besides, wasn't that what I had been doing all along?" I responded, wearily.

"Well, do it some more, especially now when your first instinct is to do, think, fix, create something more. Truly let go and see what happens in the silence, in the gap, as Deepak describes it."

I knew, of course, that Sandie was echoing back to me the very principles that both I and CosmiKids stood for—self-assuredness, living in the now, aligning with passion and keeping the faith no matter what. I had always defined faith as knowing that everything—and I do mean *everything*—is unfolding exactly as it should—even the seeming halts, missteps and, yes, the failures too; they are all part of a larger divine plan. In this situation, faith also meant letting go of control, of what I thought things *should* look like and when they should happen. Maybe I had held to this belief in the past to a lesser or greater degree but it dawned on me then that if we truly live in the present, the act of letting go is moment-to-moment, as well. I couldn't fairly say, "Well, I let go at three o'clock last Tuesday" . . . it has to be a constant process.

And for the next three days at least, it was. There in the desert, nestled in the private sanctuary of the resort with the Santa Rosa Mountains rising like sentinels around me, I relinquished all stoicism and allowed myself to hit rock bottom, to do nothing but sit in that big hole in the ground that we all retreat to when everything we believe in, everything we have been planning and building our life around has been snatched away from us—like finding out your husband has been having an affair, or that you are adopted, or that you have a fatal form of cancer. In such moments, when the whole fabric of our existence tumbles down, we may not even know who we are anymore. That's the state I was in. I didn't know who I was anymore, and it ripped at my heart because I lived and breathed Plato's mantra: "Know thyself."

"An uncomfortable feeling is not an enemy," writes author Byron Katie, whom I greatly admire and respect. "It's a gift that says, 'Get honest; inquire'." So that's what I felt I had to do. In this hole of nothingness, stripped naked of all defenses, I got brutally, honestly real with myself. I cast away the "dwelling in certainty" maxim and accepted that I had no freaking clue what was going to happen next. I didn't know anymore. I just didn't know.

Sinking further into surrender, I realized at a depth I'd never penetrated before the absolute truth and power behind the words that had become my Judy-Jude mantra: "It's not what happens to us; it's who we are going through it." Even if I walked out of that hole in the desert, went back to LA and decided to lay CosmiKids to rest forever, who would I be going through *that*? When all was said and done, would I be able to say that I had acted in such a way that I'd still have what's most important to me: my integrity, my sense of wonderment, and my connection to The One who made me exactly how I am? Sure, you can be unscrupulous and still succeed, and you can be scrupulous and not succeed. But *who do you want to be—now AND when you* do *succeed? And how do you define success anyway?*

My thoughts turned to my father, who had been kind, moral and decent as a businessman, and my mother, who had lovingly encouraged my early business ventures with words of praise and a "Judy can do" attitude. At that moment, in my hole of self-inquiry, I suddenly decided to send love to my parents, to Kim, to Cathy, to Courtney, and to all those who had taught me great lessons through CosmiKids, for reminding me that who we are (and how we treat others) is far more important than what we do.

The Indian spiritual teacher Osho once said: "I am fragile, delicate, and sensitive. That is my strength." In the end, that's how I feel about the way I came into this world, and the way in which I will leave it. My time at rock bottom was slowly revealing to me that my own personal power may reside in something quite different from the type of power that conventional society admires—as is my version of what constitutes success—but it's how I choose to be in this life. Regardless of what happens to me, or what anyone says about me, or where life's treasure map takes me, the barometer of my success is and always will be measured by the extent to which I am able to keep alive the intuitive, inquisitive, trusting child inside me. There was no way on earth I could run an organization for today's enlightened children unless I continued to honor those same qualities within me that children represent.

With that epiphany, I put my head in my hands and, finally, let the tears flow.

Once again, a welter of conflicting thoughts flooded my consciousness. *Perhaps I should just call it a day; give up, preserve what's left of my money and simply go play golf, be a lady who lunches* one part of me said.

Be honest! Another part of me taunted. *You could no more do that than give up the part of you that loves to wear edgy clothes; it wouldn't be the authentic you.*

With nowhere to turn for solace, I set my thoughts free to wander as they wished. Like a ship without a rudder, they drifted back and forth on the sea of my consciousness, until suddenly they came to rest on a miraculous incident involving my dad and my childhood that had brought me tremendous comfort and a sense of joy amidst the outer turmoil and deep questioning that had been engulfing me at that time. Back when I had been raising funds for CosmiKids, I happened to be visiting Pittsburgh during a scheduled investor presentation series. After a long day of public speaking and "being on" I had returned to my friend Deb's home to rest up a bit before we went out to dinner. I lay on her guest bed, reading the last few pages of Paulo Coelho's *The Alchemist*—a short but compelling tribute to empowered, magical thinking which at that moment in time was acting like soothing balm for my weary entrepreneurial soul. As I finished the book, I closed my eyes for an instant and briefly stroked my forehead. Suddenly, without warning, I got the clearest sense that the hand that was stroking my head did not belong to me. Instead, it had become my father's, and it was lovingly stroking my furrowed, weary brow—just like he used to do when I was small. I witnessed this odd circumstance with awe, as for several long moments, my arm no longer moved in conjunction with my own thoughts or intentions, but with those of my beloved father. Tears started pouring down my cheeks at the sheer majesty of this divine experience, and

I felt completely blessed to have been given such a miraculous glimpse of another, more expanded reality.

We have all had moments when we feel we've hit rock bottom and cannot go on a moment longer—then something happens and we find the resolve from deep within us… these are the moments when we say YES to ourselves, to something bigger and stronger than us, that then tip us over the edge into that place where everything simply flows… it's a huge choice point. That's what happened to me when I was convinced I felt my father reach out to me across the divide. I have no doubt that everything that came after that particular moment, came BECAUSE of the choice I made in that instant. For all at once, in a moment that seemed like an eternity, yet passed in an instant, a profound sense of peace washed over me and wiped clean my deepest layer of sadness. In its place rushed forth feelings of worthiness, deservedness, renewed conviction of purpose and—last but not least—tremendous waves of gratitude. As always, I knew that my heart would tell itself what to do, and I would heed its wisdom, whatever it was.

And so I made my choice; to trust, to go on, and to continue to follow my dream and my passion. So long as I continued to take one step at a time, I would be shown the next one, and the next one, and I would be supported in ways beyond my imagining.

Lounging under a shady cabana in the hours before our departure from Miramonte, I reflected with a more balanced perspective on the situation with Courtney. It occurred to me that another valued outcome of that situation was my deepening understanding that everything, and I mean *everything*, is a process. Learning how to keep my heart open in a business world where many people could and would take advantage of this has been—and continues to be—an enormous life lesson for me. And continually working through this so I can reach my own fullest potential is *also* a process. Our emotional, psychological or spiritual lessons—whatever they may be—are a process, as well. And it is as we heal through each layer of the onion that we meet with success of the truest kind.

My time in the ring with Courtney may have been called on a technicality, but in my book, we had both come out of it as winners. I cannot speak for Courtney but I know that she is intelligent and aware enough to interpret the gifts in this for herself. For my part, one of the many things that Courtney taught me was to always stand in my truth, no matter how painful and no matter what the outcome. As Byron Katie says in *A Thousand Names for Joy: Living in Harmony With the Way Things Are*: "Of course, freedom doesn't mean that you let unkind things happen—it doesn't mean passivity or masochism. If someone says he's going to cut off your legs, run!"

I'll never have the killer instinct but I know now that I shouldn't lie down and simply take what doesn't feel right for me, or compromise who I am. Courtney and I never did sign a formal business contract but I'm certain that on another level, she had lovingly agreed to enter into a more important contract with me in this lifetime: to challenge me to be the best that I can be. That's the mark of a true friend, and for that I will always be grateful to her.

20.

The Phoenix Rises

Like a sunrise after a tsunami, like a rainbow after the storm, I arrived back in LA to find that after living and loving Deepak's Laws of Success for so many years, and believing in the supreme intelligence of the universe, the tide inevitably started to turn for me—and in its wake came the most amazing gifts.

In the weeks and months after my return from the desert I couldn't help but notice that many of my deepest wishes, prayers, whimsies, imaginings and long-held goals—all the way back to the beginning of Kids at Heart so many years before—now came boomeranging back to me in ways that were even greater than I had ever imagined or intended. Suddenly, everything was different. It didn't feel as if I was doing much of anything in terms of taking any specific actions to make these things happen, yet all of a sudden, people were seeking me out with their ideas and reaching out to me for collaboration and co-creation.

What had happened to change things? As I had learned from Deepak very early on, my intentions were now magically organizing their own fulfillment. With hindsight, I could see that my time in the desert had been necessary for me to master (at least in terms of my business venture) the concept of detachment. According to Deepak, "Detachment is synonymous with wealth consciousness, because with detachment there is freedom to create." For too long, I had been fixated only on the franchise model and opening a test site. In the process I had partially lost sight of something essential: the ability to view the bigger picture and endlessly go with the flow. Yes, I was happily floating along in my cosmic bubble, but as special as our Hollywood six-month run had been, I now realized, I had still been thinking too small. I needed to think *outside* the bubble. I remembered one of our basic CosmiKids tenets: that the cosmic divine consists of not just one but countless spheres of possibility, and keeping an open mind *at all times* is what leads us to pure potential, which can reveal itself *in any given moment*. If we do not stay aware and in the present, these bubbles can pass straight by our consciousness, unnoticed and unappreciated.

Coming Full Circle

Deepak's teachings had initially inspired me to move to California, and the Chopra Center for Well Being had served as an exquisite launch platform for CosmiKids. So I was absolutely delighted when, in a serendipitous twist of events, I was suddenly approached to appear in a movie based on Deepak's best-selling book, *Seven Spiritual Laws of Success*, distributed by 20th Century Fox Films. When Deepak's daughter, Mallika, a film producer, discovered CosmiKids and the new paradigm philosophies behind it, she said, "Judy, you are truly living the essence of the *Seven Spiritual Laws*. We would like you to be a part of our upcoming film project." So, there I am, alongside Olivia Newton-John, Dave Stewart of the Eurythmics and others who live and breathe these spiritual principles.

Then, out of the blue, I was handed another grand opportunity to do one of my favorite things: share these spiritual principles with others in a public forum. As the designated spokesperson for the movie, I embarked on a bi-coastal tour with The Learning Annex, the premier producer of seminars, lectures, classes and workshops throughout the U.S. and Canada, to speak about the very tenets that elevated my spirit and fueled my dharma seven years ago. To me, it's all an example of the Law of Attraction in motion...and in motion pictures!

From the time I produced the *MeToo* pilot for Kids at Heart in the 1980s, I've always dreamed of translating "consciousness for kids" into a children's television program. The next thrilling piece of synchronicity occurred when I was contacted by one of the very companies that define children's entertainment, with whom we have subsequently been discussing ideas for a CosmiKids-inspired children's television show.

And, just in case you need any more proof of synchronicity, divine intervention or the power of intention, here's another delicious twist of the "you-couldn't-make-it-up-if-you-tried" variety:

Just as Sandie and I were leaving Miramonte, I had shared with her another intention: to manifest a seasoned business advisor and financial strategist to partner with who could help me take CosmiKids where it is destined to go as a financially viable, sustainable organization. And, you bet, my biggest criteria for this person was. . . someone I could trust, someone with integrity through and through. Where would I find them?

As luck would have it (or synchronicity), my very first partner and soul sister, Jennifer, and her husband, John, had just completed an amazing period in their own lives as entrepreneurs. They had worked together for many years and had met with such overwhelming success that they were now able to take early retirement. I would never have imagined that John might be interested in aligning with CosmiKids... until Sandie presciently voiced the possibility, thereby prompting a conversation that resulted in a partnership the like of which even I hadn't dared to dream.

John is now serving as our co-CEO, with Jennifer as our CFO and board member, along with me and Sandie, who, in another strange and serendipitous turn of fate, unexpectedly moved back to California, thus paving the way for a number of intentions that she and I had been setting over the years to fall magically into place. John asks the hard questions, looks at the big picture, devises creative, innovative solutions for growth, articulates financial strategies, and doesn't forget to add in some fun dinners at wonderful LA restaurants when he's out on the west coast working with us. Although he and Jennifer live in Pittsburgh and Hyannis, Cape Cod, they find time to convene regularly on conference calls, join us in person for important meetings and otherwise keep in close contact via emails.

With John and Jen's encouragement, and Sandie's insights about additional cutting edge programs that CosmiKids could be developing and offering to families and children alongside our Discovery Stations experiences, we took the decision to open our flagship company-owned CosmiKids neighborhood location in Tarzana, California in the summer of 2007.

John also introduced us to Shaun, a wonderful merger and acquisitions specialist, who is now helping us formulate effective strategies for growth. This southern-bred attorney with an impressive yet conservative background genuinely believes we are onto something BIG, and feels we've done a "truly remarkable job of branding and positioning such a New Thought idea in a mainstream, acceptable way"—which is certainly a far cry from the pronouncements issued by Courtney's consultants!

As a true testament to the power of intention setting, synchronicity, co-creation and manifestation, here I am at last, with the wonderful executive team I had always envisioned and have now intended into being—John,

Jen, Sandie, Shaun—every single one of them brilliant, trusted, passionate and totally committed to all the principles and philosophies that are so integral to the foundation of CosmiKids and everything it stands for.

At last, my dream has come true. As if on cue, and thanks in part to the interest generated by my appearance in Deepak's movie, together with the prolific media coverage CosmiKids is getting for its groundbreaking new programs and cutting edge concepts at our flagship location, we are now being flooded with calls from people around the globe interested in opening franchise locations. Our hands are full and our hearts are soaring.

Through all of this and more, I continue to set the daily intention to impact the way we educate our youth in a powerful and positive way, to replicate cosmic play spaces around the world in which children, parents and teachers can explore new ways of being together—connecting to the heart and from the soul, viewing the child as teacher, and holding a precious light for the fullest expression of human potential that any generation has ever known.

Meantime, we are together actively co-creating even more innovative ways to enable communities to connect with one another and educate the hearts of families and children. While Sandie and I are busy developing more pioneering programs designed to assist children in developing their emotional IQ, and creating our own line of original and innovative empowerment products—including a brand new family magazine called *Inspired Parenting*—John and Jen are focusing their energies on establishing a non-profit foundation that will enable us to offer all of our programs, products and services free to children and families who might not otherwise be in a position to afford them.

It's taken a few stops, starts and pauses, but at last, my dream of founding a purpose-driven company with kids at its heart is now a reality.

Ahh . . . Finally, Kids at Heart has come full circle!

21.

In the Pink

So, what is the undeniable lesson that brought me to this wonderful place of being able to both live *and* love success in the moment? It is simply this: be true to who you are. We all have naysayers in our lives, and I firmly believe that we meet with success when we find the courage to refuse to conform to others' expectations of us and, instead, do what our hearts are calling us to do. I have one final story to tell that recently reminded me of this important lesson in a big (and colorful!) way.

Sandie and I were standing on the upper balcony of the famous Arc Light Theatre on Hollywood's Sunset Strip, enjoying the view and discussing the movie we had just seen. While overlooking the crowd of people below us, I noticed some buying movie tickets, others having a bite to eat or milling around enjoying the gift shop and memorabilia kiosks. Then all at once I spotted a gal with gorgeous light pink hair.

"Hey!" I remarked to Sandie. "Look at her cool hair!"

We both acknowledged how good the girl's hair looked, and how bold she was to choose such a distinctive color.

"You know, that color would look really good on you, Judy," Sandie said.

"What?" I asked, unsure whether she was joking or not.

"Really," she insisted. "I mean it. If anyone can wear pink hair, it's you!"

"Ohhhhh…" I breathed, trying on the idea for size. Well, I had a hair appointment scheduled for the following week. On a whim, I dialed my stylist's number and told her what I was contemplating.

"Judy, that would be so totally, uniquely you!" she said.

Six days later, Sandie, Tina (the hair stylist) and I were sitting in my apartment, surveying my new hairdo… which hadn't turned out *quite* like

I'd expected. Instead of the soft blush pink I'd envisioned, I was now sporting a day-glow halo. Tina tried adding more bleach to tone it down a few notches, but it was still vivid pink.

"Hmmm," I murmured. "You know, I'm wondering if this is a little bit too much, even for me."

Sandie cocked her head on one side, considering. "Actually, I rather like it." She finally pronounced.

"So do I," concurred Tina.

I got up to look in the mirror. Yep, it was certainly bright all right. But something about it was beginning to grow on me.

"Oh well," I said. "I guess I'm going to be in the pink for a while."

"It will certainly make you stand out among all the usual presenters at the Learning Annex," Sandie added.

Oh my gosh! The Learning Annex!

"Oh-h-h-h-h s-h-i-t! I wasn't thinking about my seminar next week." I wailed. "What will people think? What will they say? Will anyone take me seriously with shocking pink hair?"

"Relax, Judy. This couldn't be more perfect, don't you see?" Sandie smiled. Having worked with me on the structure and content of my seminar, Sandie knew better than anyone exactly how different I planned my seminar to be. But in that moment, I wasn't quite so sure. I mean, I was really growing to love my pink hair, but would the people paying to attend my seminars find the vibrancy of the shade to be a little too far out there?

As the week wore on, my concern began to subside as more and more people stopped me on the street to tell me how much they loved my hair. Granted, the majority of them were between the ages of 13 and 30, but still, quite a few older people were nodding and smiling, and one or two had even said they wish they'd had the guts to do it. But I still had a smidgen of doubt about whether it was the thing for a seminar presenter to be sporting. But what the heck—it wasn't as if I could do anything about it at this stage, according to Tina.

The evening of the seminar arrived, and with it came faint stirrings of nervousness. *Perhaps I should counteract the effect of my hair with a nice, conventional staid suit,* I considered. Rifling through my closet, I surveyed its eclectic contents. *A conventional suit?* Who was I kidding? The words "conventional," "staid" and "suit" didn't apply to anything in my closet. So, I reached past the1950s taffeta ball gown, the multicolored sequined scarves and rhinestone accessories, and pulled out one of my favorite, most comfortable quirky outfits.

Then it occurred to me: everything that people had been telling me all week (and I had been telling myself all my life) suddenly coalesced into a blaring epiphany. It was perfect! The hair... the wardrobe... every bit of it was absolutely perfect. Why? Because it was me. Whether others love it or hate it, it all authentically reflected me. It's like the saying I once heard and loved so much that I wrote it down and taped it to my bathroom mirror:

Just be yourself.

Nobody can tell you you're doing it wrong.

So, pinking out my hair wasn't just a whim, after all. It was the universe reminding me once again that it was co-creating every step of the way with me, offering me opportunities to be myself in my fullest expression. I believe that's how the universe operates; it co-creates with us in myriad small and large ways—by showing me that gal at the movie theater, for instance. And all we have to do is be open to receiving its messages. If there's one thing I have learned from looking back on my life it's that over and over again, synchronicity—those meaningful coincidences that Carl Jung wrote about—has formed the links in the chain that have directed my path. Everything—and everyone—is linked. It's no accident that I've had the experiences I've had. And it's no mistake that you are reading this book right now.

My journey towards my true life purpose and the creation of CosmiKids began at a stop light in Pittsburgh, when I knew deep within me that there was an important movement going on in the world and I wanted to be a part of it. I could also say that it began as a young girl, as I watched the way my father conducted himself in the business world and how he thoughtfully imparted his entrepreneurial perspectives of possibility to his young, impressionable daughter. In truth, my journey, like yours, began the moment I started to construct a story for myself about myself. And, like everyone's journey, it begins again and again with each new experience we encounter, if we look with fresh, innocent eyes.

Life is an adventure, a story with limitless potential, and we are the authors, the artists, the sole crafters of our own stories. Whether we turn that story into a comedy, a drama, a tragedy, a soap opera, a love story, or a triumph, is entirely up to us. And we have the power to change it any time. What's more, I've learned that each chapter in our lives is another opportunity for us to learn and grow, to live and love, and to incorporate our findings into our own personal version of a successful life. And speaking of success, I believe there is really only one common denominator among all of us in terms of what constitutes true "success": it is living each moment being true to who you are, knowing what makes you tick and what keeps you "in the pink". It is also believing in the heights you can reach and, within that pure potential, daring to flirt with the future—the future that is uniquely yours to create. There is no limit to the heights you can reach because all potential resides within you.

My journey became my school and my school became the tools that I used to craft a life of purpose (many of these tools have been highlighted throughout the book). As I moved forward in crafting a life that is authentic to me, I gained inspiration along the way from many sources—most importantly, many "little" sources: the children with whom I've gleefully interacted over the years at CosmiKids. I continue to learn from them every day. In fact, if my life philosophy were to be called "child's play", I would take this as the highest form of flattery because children live and love in the best possible way. They are continuously open to discovering new things; they live more authentically than most adults! When watching children at CosmiKids, I'm continually amazed at their boundless ability to stretch their imaginations to new heights. For example, one day, a rock in the garden could be a boat; another day, it might be a throne; another day, a mountain.

I believe that children are creative and unbounded in this way because they have a quality of innocence that enables them to turn everything in their imagination into something else that serves the story they are playing out in that moment. As adults, it's sometimes a challenge to stay open to the wonder, whimsy and unexpected nature of existence. But what if we grownups started greeting everything with an open mind, as children do? What epiphanies, miracles and breakthroughs might await us if we could "forget" what we think we know and started behaving as if both our possibilities and potential are limitless? After all, what do we *really* have to lose? Nothing but old worn-out ways of being.

One of the tools that I've found helpful is to say to myself, *I am willing to see things differently in this moment.* I'm always surprised at what transpires.

Another thing that continually inspires me about children is their capacity to forgive—both themselves and others. You can punish or scold them one day and it's the end of the world as far as they're concerned, and the next day, they are so willing to let it go. They have exactly the same attitude towards failure. Think of a two-year-old who is just learning to tie his shoes. If he doesn't succeed at first, he doesn't give up; he just keeps on trying to perfect that knot. Then one day, when all the conditions are right—when he has developed the necessary dexterity and given it enough practice—he masters it and achieves success. Any success in life is a process, a moment—to-moment trust and an occasional big leap of faith. So go easy on yourself. Stop thinking of 'fail' as a four-letter word. All 'failure' means is that the conditions aren't quite right yet. We all have highs and lows and even stops. (Goodness knows I had 25 years of stops, starts and pauses!) Honor them. If you use these times to quiet your mind and connect with your inner voice, you will find that the right answer is always waiting. And when we listen attentively to our inner wisdom, we cannot fail.

What Would *You* Do If You Knew You Could Not Fail?

Which leads me to conclude my story with this question to you:

What if… every decision you make is supremely correct?

What if… you knew you couldn't fail? What incredible things might you be capable of doing that are *totally and uniquely you*?

What would truly put you in the pink…fully expressing the essence of who you are?

This book is my story. I am living proof that anyone, and I mean *anyone*, can manifest their dreams. It's all in the believing that we really do have the power to create our own reality and manifest magic and miracles in every single area of our life.

Now it's time to start living *your* story. But first, you have to write it. Not the story you've been living, but the one that you've been dreaming. I'd like to help you if you'll let me. At the end of this book there are several blank pages. I invite you to take a few moments to examine them. Note how clean, pristine and full of promise they are. These pages are my gift to you. They represent your future, a story that's just waiting to be written. It's the story of who you really are, and the bold, bright thing you would do if you knew you could not fail.

And if you don't yet know what that might be, let me ask you this: What wild, glorious, utterly audacious dream can you envision that would truly set your heart singing? Regardless of how fanciful or unrealistic it might seem, I'm going to ask you to take that dream and project it out in front of you, as if you were watching it on a full-size movie screen. Make the colors brighter, the picture bigger, the focus sharper. Then step into the center of it and imagine what it would be like to *really live this dream.*

Now pick up a pencil and write it all down. Fill these blank pages with as many details as you can. Make a record of your dream, breathe life into it, listen to the song of it, let yourself be guided and inspired by the rhythm of it.

Fall in love with it.

Claim it.

Dare to dream it into being, and start romancing *your* future.

After doing so, please meet me again on page 209...

Of course, as with every real life drama, which doesn't end when the lovers are reunited, or the athlete triumphs over adversity to win Olympic gold, my story isn't over. This tale is still playing out. And because my story is about following one's inner guidance system, and daring to live outside the box, I really couldn't do anything other than continue to allow it to unfold in real time beyond the final page.

I invite you to accompany me as both witness and companion as I continue to "romance my future" (and the future of CosmiKids) via whatever interactive means technology affords us—including videos, forums and blogs—on my website at **www.judyjulin.com**, where I'll also be sharing more details of all the tools, techniques and principles that I've mentioned throughout this book.

I look forward to meeting you personally online!

FINDHORN PRESS

Books, Card Sets,
CDs & DVDs
that inspire and uplift

For a complete catalogue,
please contact:

Findhorn Press Ltd
305a The Park, Findhorn
Forres IV36 3TE
Scotland, UK

Telephone +44-(0)1309-690582
Fax +44-(0)1309-690036
eMail info@findhornpress.com

or consult our catalogue online
(with secure order facility) on
www.findhornpress.com